social

work

practice:

a response

to the

urban

crisis

carol h. meyer

COLLIER–MACMILLAN LIMITED, LONDON

social work practice: a response to the urban crisis

THE FREE PRESS, NEW YORK

Collier-Macmillan Canada Ltd., Toronto, Ontario

Library of Congress Catalog Card Number: 72–124641

printing number
5   6   7   8   9   10

preface

The future is not an overreaching leap into
the distance; it begins in the present.

——Daniel Bell[1]

THIS IS A BOOK about the practice of social
work in the present increasingly urban, industrialized, and
impersonal society. It is addressed primarily to the social
welfare scene in the United States, but it also may be relevant in part to those places elsewhere that are confronting
the same kinds of pressures of city life in a mechanized and
bureaucratized world. It is a book written in the present,
on the threshold of the last quarter of the 20th century, but
it reflects the immediate past and it presumes to comment
upon how social work will or may have to be practiced in
the future.

A word about the form of the book. One of the most
difficult tasks confronting students of the modern social
scene is that of limitation: the need to set boundaries to
the range of ideas so that they will not flood the mind.
Once having set those boundaries, one is still compelled to
deal with too many components at once and finally must
select only the most pertinent issues out of the morass of
bombarding stimuli.

One way to achieve a sense of orderliness is to discuss
issues on the highest possible level of abstraction, because

---

[1] Bell, Daniel, *Toward the Year 2000: Work in Progress, Daedalus,*
Summer 1967, p. 639.

up there in the thin air almost everyone could agree; there would be few distractions. However, as soon as one attempts to apply ideas and make them practical it becomes extremely difficult, because then one has, alas, to deal with the intrusion of reality.

In an effort to enlarge the parameters of the ensuing discussion and to make it applicable for the social work practitioner, the choice has been made to follow a very old dictum in social work, which is to start where we are. Occasionally, it will be necessary to recall the historical development of an idea, and it will be helpful as well to reach in our imagination for abstractions that leap beyond the present reality. But the framework for the book will be the current issues with which the field of social work is coping. The bibliography will list references that describe the field and explain the techniques of its practitioners, but the form and substance of this book must of necessity be bent to the statement the author is trying to make. It cannot cover everything, but it must always be made relevant to the current social scene to which it is addressed. It is then a book that attempts to be theoretical but not abstract; it seeks to be present and future oriented, while not unmindful of historical explanations; it tries to be reflective of the real and present world, but not, we hope, pedestrian, nor concerned with technicalities.

The form of the book is as follows:

CHAPTER 1 is about the critical state of social work practice in 1969. It deals with popular notions of what social workers are, with students' quests for relevant practice, with social scientists' arguments about its appropriateness, and with organizational responses to social work's failures.

CHAPTER 2 explores what went wrong with the excellent theoretical developments in social casework; were they faulty, or were they misunderstood and misapplied?

CHAPTER 3 is concerned with the urban condition, with social upheaval and changing power alignments that define the nature of social programs.

CHAPTER 4 describes the changes in traditional and favored social institutions like the family, and the increasing impact of public health, education, and welfare services.

CHAPTER 5 discusses the big issue of individualization in the present urban scene. It examines issues of knowledge and practice that are thought to be most urgent in updating social work practice.

CHAPTER 6 contains proposals for social intervention that derive from our view of the urban scene and newer models of individualization.

CHAPTER 7 explores the vital manpower issues that need to be resolved, in order to make modern social work practice adaptive to the urban situation.

contents

social

work

practice:

a response

to the

urban

crisis

1

the critical state of social work practice

*These people just have in their minds that
if you come and ask them a question you are a
social worker or someone from the government
checking up on them. They're on the defensive.*
——N.Y. Times, Nov. 1, 1968[2]

---

[2] *N.Y. Times*, Nov. 1, 1968, "Gallup Scraps Harlem Poll Because of False Data."

IT SEEMS TO BE the lot of social workers that they are always under criticism. The people they serve— the clients and patients of health and welfare agencies— seem to feel unserved; the public at large and the press often express judgments that social workers do too little— or too much—for their clientele; professional colleagues in other disciplines may argue that they could do better through their methods; social workers themselves and students in graduate schools of social work are vocal about the question of the relevancy of social work practice in today's world.

There are at least four large issues that seem to be at the core of the criticisms of social work practice. Until these issues are aired and settled, the best that social workers do through their practice will never be good enough. Confusion over the stance to be taken on the following questions may account for the high degree of public and self-criticism about social work practice.

The problem seems to derive largely from a confusion of aims and methods and from the special types of affiliations that social workers must make with social problems and social institutions. It has been said that when something goes wrong, the community tends to attack the organization rather than the cause. Perhaps this tendency has to do with the greater visibility of the organization and the elusive quality of causation.

We perceive the misunderstandings to rise from these concerns:

1. The halting development of social services, from charity to public welfare.

2. The association of social work practice with the social ills that afflict society.

3. The pull between the aims of practice and those of social change.

4. The drive toward professionalization and specialization.

Naturally, our discussion must rest in an understanding of the nature of our present urban society and the rapid and radical changes that are occurring throughout the world. It is the changing social scene that has brought the criticism of social work into bold relief; in an earlier day the practice of social work was more consonant with the pace of the times and the clearer definitions of political and social class power structures. The thesis of this book is that social work practice could become significant to the welfare of people in the present day of social turmoil, but that the purposes and the boundaries of that practice must be reconceptualized. One of the most important qualities of social work is that it, perhaps more than any field of practice, is systemically related to the social scene. It is a reflection of the forces in society. When those forces are forward-looking, so is social work. Of course when those social forces turn inward and become reactionary, social work as one of society's institutions will also follow that course. Social work may devise and influence social programs; it may lead people toward rational social policy, or it may help its clientele to confront irrational systems, but it remains a function of society at large; it has no laboratory in which it can control its practice without reference to surrounding conditions.

We shall see as this book unfolds that there is a function for social work that could be more syntonic with the times in which we live. Practice need not be tied to clinical definitions of cases in order to be effective, and, in fact, cases themselves need not remain insular in order to be identifiable. Furthermore, social workers need not be desk-bound in order to be expert, nor must professionals perform every task in every case action in order to maintain high levels of service. The world has relaxed, and social work practice as a social institution reflective of that world must relax as well. If social work practice does not closely follow the life style of this present civilization, social work services will become meaningless and practice will atrophy. We will propose that the primary purpose of social work practice is to individualize people in the mass urban society, but first, we need to examine some of the causes for the present critical state of social work practice.

THE HALTING DEVELOPMENT OF SOCIAL SERVICES FROM CHARITY TO WELFARE

The present revolution in the streets and on the campuses is addressed to a variety of specific issues, but always the cry of youth, the black militants, and the organized poor is about "the establishment." The establishment differs according to the issue being confronted. Whereas the Pentagon is the relevant establishment for a peace march, the university plays that role for angry students, and the local board of education serves to rally discontented neighborhood parent groups. In the social welfare arena, the Welfare Rights Organization perceives the local department of welfare as the establishment. Were the clientele of family and child welfare agencies and medical and psychiatric patients to organize, they too would seek their particular "establishment" to confront. Thus, the fact that social workers work for social agencies and participate in the carrying out of prevalent social policies unquestionably associates them with "the establishment."

Because the term establishment has come to have a pejorative meaning, it creates a sense of embarrassment for practitioners in social work who are so often appropriately identified with the underdog and with the very groups who are prepared to upset the establishment with which they are concerned. A specific organization that is supported by public or private funds generally will not be under the auspices and administrative control of social work practitioners themselves, and the young social worker will then find companionship with the clientele that is organizing against the agency. The paradox that arises from this kind of situation is all too obvious: Organizations are unlikely to support the forces that seek their downfall, and reality demands that the practitioner on the payroll of an agency make a choice as to his own affiliations. We are not here taking sides in the struggle about whether or not establishments are good or bad; we are only commenting upon their inevitability, for it has been true historically that when an old establishment is overthrown a new one rises up to take its place. Today, whether the establishment be government, education, health, or welfare, it is an object of popular disdain. Things are not going right in our world, and people must hold the varied establishments responsible for their plight. Thus, no matter how well social workers might practice, they will suffer the onslaughts that are heaped upon the establishments for which they work.

The white middle-class sectarian characteristics of voluntary agencies and of the limited professional staff employed in public agencies has also become a contentious issue in the present day of power realignments. The development of voluntary agencies in this country came out of the Elizabethan poor law matrix and the Judeo-Christian roots of charity. Humanitarian impulses and those religious concerns that were associated with saving the soul of the giver motivated the provision of voluntary social services in the 18th and 19th centuries.[3] Sectarianism was integral to the idea of voluntarism, because when groups of private citizens joined in an organized effort to cope with family and child welfare problems especially, their common purpose was to care for their own. It is a primitive and fundamental characteristic of all ethnically bound people that

[3] Klein, Philip, *From Philanthropy to Social Welfare,* Jossey-Bass Inc., San Francisco, Calif., 1968, Chap. XVI, "Theoretical-Philosophic Foundations," pp. 269–290.

Lubove, Roy, *The Professional Altruist,* Harvard University Press, Cambridge, Mass., 1965, Chap. 1, "Charity Organization and the New Gospel of Benevolence," pp. 1–21.

Mencher, Samuel, *Poor Law to Poverty Program,* University of Pittsburgh Press, Pittsburgh, Pa., 1967, Chap. 6, "The Reform of the Poor Law . . . The Ideological Background," pp. 93–98.

Woodroofe, Kathleen, *From Charity to Social Work,* University of Toronto Press, Toronto, Canada, 1962, Chap. IV, "Poverty and Oysters in the U.S.A.," pp. 77–100.

they will seek ways of continuing their clan. As religious groups evolved separately and in different eras in this country, voluntarism, sectarianism, and separatism became characteristic of the first welfare efforts.

One example of the development of the lag between voluntarism and the welfare of the general public can be seen in the field of child welfare, although one might use any of the social work fields of practice to describe the route taken in the 20th century from charity to welfare. On the East Coast, where the American settlement brought along the English model of voluntary services, child welfare organizations developed in response to the worsening conditions brought about by industrialization. The influence of Protestant, Catholic, and Jewish voluntary social agencies in eastern states is well known, as each took care of their own groups to the extent that their own referential communities could afford to provide quality services. The influence upon social welfare of these sectarian agencies was so vast that, when public facilities developed as a more realistic response to the universal condition of children in industrialized families, these organizations remained in positions to authoritatively influence the programs of public agencies as well as their own. The tripartite division of voluntary agencies served their function for almost a century, and might have continued to do so but for the incursion of certain mid-20th century realities.

The urban crisis occurred, or at least became apparent to the public at large. This meant that black and other minority people were intent upon being counted as having need for services, and the extent of need expanded beyond any voluntary agency's capacity to cope with it. As occurred when other ethnic groups developed their sectarian agencies, the line of development in the modern scene might have been the addition of a black nonsectarian type of voluntary agency to provide social services to their own people. However, blacks were not themselves well enough organized, nor sufficiently endowed financially to make such a direction of effort feasible. Typically then, the public agency through its child welfare services became the primary social agency for black families. Racial characteristics became a differentiating factor that outweighed the religious factors. Thus therapeutic institutional facilities might be uncrowded by children of one religious (white) group and yet be unavailable to the black child who needed them, and the black child would be confined to an overcrowded public children's shelter. Or the adoption agencies would seek adoptable babies for their clientele, and black adoptable babies would remain in congregate care. This anachronistic situation has been mitigated somewhat by the rise of public social welfare services, but in the course of the voluntary agency era, social work practice flourished, developed its methods, carried out the defined programs, became professionalized and didn't notice that the urban crisis had erupted.

The development of *public welfare agencies* in this country was spurred by the Depression and the New Deal of the Roosevelt era and was designed to cope with the effects of the social failures of industrialism. Once again in American history it became evident that unemployment and poverty were not caused by personal failure, because the entire world was suffering from economic want. Not only were voluntary agencies no longer able to afford the mounting costs of economic provision for their client groups, but also during this period it became apparent that economic security was a public responsibility because it was recognized that the society had failed.[4] The welfare of the public became a political issue, and the charitable age began to diminish, although it never completely disappeared. The changing role of government in the social and economic affairs of citizens gradually influenced the public to consider that social and economic failure was a concomitant of the kind of society in which people lived and not the result of personal failure. In the ensuing thirty years, from the

---

[4] Schlesinger, Arthur M., Jr., *The Coming of the New Deal*, Houghton Mifflin Co., New York, 1958, Chap. 16, "The Rise of Federal Relief," pp. 263–281.

1930s to the 1960s, welfare became an enlarged concept to include mental health services, family and child welfare programs, medicare programs, research into the diseases of modern civilization, and social insurance against naturally expected risks of living in an industrialized world. Thus, whereas public welfare originally was concerned primarily with economic welfare, the term has evolved into something that might be called services for the public's welfare—a final assumption by government of provisions of service and care, economic supports and research into basic causes of physical, mental, and social pathologies.

Naturally, the vast scope of health, education, and welfare services made necessary a large bureaucratic organization in the structure of the Department of Health, Education, and Welfare (HEW). Much as voluntary organizations found it increasingly impossible to cope through money and staff with the newly defined client or citizen group requiring services, so did local public organizations in states, counties and municipalities find federally determined need on a broad scale to exert pressure upon the local units of service. It was one thing for federal policy to state that all citizens should have a decent standard of living and quite another for subsidiary governmental structures to be able to afford to make such provisions. But for thirty years, even as federal programs enlarged, and costs were shared, state and cities were burdened with the costs and implementation, until finally the sheer weight of advancement in health and welfare programs created overwhelming burdens for the state and local agencies. Public service agencies grew into bureaucratic monsters as they tried to keep up with federal mandates while often struggling with local or state funds and inadequate federal funding.

When an office of the social insurance program grows in the size of its clientele or the scope of its provisions, it is relatively simple, organizationally speaking, to add a number of clerical or semi-administrative staff to the office and to expand the computer services of the agency. More space, more staff, more money might be needed, but the basic form of the service does not change and require new personnel arrangements or innovative service devices. However, in the case of public assistance, when the Congress legislates a medical or social service program that involves differences in form and relies on changes in quality of service, this is no longer a question of more services: structures must be reevaluated and redrawn in order to reconceptualize the service. Perhaps one of the reasons for the present entanglement of public welfare services and confusion in guidelines for personnel that provide the services has to do with the mistaken notion that adding more of anything makes a difference in the delivery of those services. An analogy may be found in looking at the modern drugstore, forced by a public responding to advertising, that adds to its shelves every new product that is devised in the cosmetic industry. There finally comes a time when the addition of hair sprays, soaps, and lipsticks makes it impossible for the shelves to hold anything else. Ultimately, the druggist must sit down and rethink his inventory procedures; he must either decide to select among the offerings, to give priority to one over the other, to sell more of one product and less of another, or to group them all differently, so that he will have a category of cosmetics that he can keep track of and handle efficiently. Analogously, this is the problem facing modern public welfare agencies.

When a public social agency is mandated to provide money, family counseling, job training, foster care, adoption, protective services, homemaking services, day care and so on, it will finally burst at the seams with the continuing addition of staff, costs, administrative duplications, and the like. At some point, it must reassess its functions, consolidating some, rearranging others, giving some priorities, exchanging others. This has not occurred in this country, and the public service agencies have, to all intents and purposes, begun to strangle in their own network of services. The role of professional social work practice in public agencies has been minimal, particularly when compared with its presence in voluntary agencies.[5] Thus, while this country turned in the direction of assuming public responsibility for the welfare of its citizens, professional social workers were barely represented in public welfare agencies. Once again, it must be assumed that social work practitioners didn't notice that the world was changing.

The 1960s found the public welfare agencies in a serious squeeze between bureaucratic suffocation and extreme public pressure for the services they were mandated by law to provide. The poverty programs of the Kennedy and Johnson administrations were, in a large sense, a response to this impasse and so evolved a new organizational era, of which the *locally devised, federally supported project* was the hallmark. In the effort to bypass what appeared to be the hopeless paralysis of established voluntary and public agencies and in order to meet the increasingly vocal demand of black, Hispanic, and Mexican-American people in the cities who were not receiving their rightful services or the income maintenance that was held out to them, poverty projects that reached directly from the local communities to the federally supported Office of Economic Opportunity (OEO) became a common device for funding of services. The inclusion of the provision for maximum feasible participation of the poor in their own community projects enhanced the popularity for this form of public support of social services, for in some ways it was an ideal opportunity for people to cope directly with their own affairs.

The matter of community control is not a modern urban phenomenon, but its form differs markedly from the older town meeting. Sometimes popular demand is misunderstood to be a crisis in itself, that community people are demanding their rights to a decent income and social services, but the crisis may be rather in the halting process of government in providing people with their needs and their rights. The sense of community, whether expressed through

---

[5] National Social Welfare Assembly and U.S. Dept. of Labor, Bureau of Labor Statistics, *Salaries and Working Conditions of Social Welfare Manpower in 1960*, New York, 1961, p. 1.

demands in local community-controlled schools or through community-of-interest groups for higher public assistance allowances, more flexible clinic hours, or more accessible social workers, may, indeed, become the very safety valve that will provide for all citizens in urban America the personal affiliation necessary to compensate for the sense of urban isolation. Yet the essence of community participation and control has been antithetical to the professional practice of social work, and professional social workers, by design, have played a limited role in the poverty programs of the 1960s.

Writing in the Foreword of their study on *Dilemmas of Social Reform*, Marris and Rein[6] say that although the Community Action Program (CAP), the precursor of the War on Poverty as a movement of reform, was

> . . . concerned with poverty, it arose less from protest or moral indignation at injustice, than from a sense of breakdown in the institutions which should be diffusing opportunities to all.

In his recent book, *Commitment to Welfare*, Richard Titmuss[7] describes the roots of the Poverty Program in the same fashion, saying that:

> The strategy attempted was basically a shortcut; a series of programmes to by-pass the established structures of power, governmental, state and local; to reach the poor directly and concentrate resources on them without the support of an infrastructure of social welfare utilized by the non-poor as well as the poor.

Both books have a great deal to say about existing bureaucracies and about the specification of programs for the poor, who were expected to stand up and announce themselves and, through maximum feasible participation, to fare better

---

[6] Marris, Peter and Rein, Martin, *Dilemmas of Social Reform*, Atherton Press, New York, 1967, p. 1.

[7] Titmuss, Richard M., *Commitment to Welfare*, Pantheon Books, Random House, New York, 1968, p. 113.

than through their past reliance upon "welfare bureaucracies." We shall not deal analytically here with the War on Poverty, except to consider it as one of a host of organized criticisms against the welfare establishment and thereby the social work practitioner as an integral part of that establishment. We must take for granted the basic competition of OEO with the HEW organization "across the street." It was true that the poor people of our country were not becoming part of the on-going life of their communities, that they were, indeed, left out, and pushed out of the opportunity structure which would hold out from them jobs, housing, medical care, education, and social services.[8] According to these experts and others, the War on Poverty was an interesting political program that intended to involve people in their own destinies in a dynamic way. There was an assumed commitment to puritan concepts on the part of the existing social welfare establishment and a belief that social welfare bureaucracies were hopelessly rigid and unimaginative, so new organizations were devised in order to cope with the dysfunctional agencies. Thus, VISTA, Peace Corps, CAP, Operation Headstart, and the Job Corps, among other programs, became the innovative agencies of the early 1960s.

Beyond political reasons, the major OEO programs also seemed to be reactive against civil service and "traditional" social work methods as the conservative agents of the faulty social institutions. Had the poverty programs succeeded, we might have a different kind of social welfare establishment today, but unfortunately according to some critics they held out more promise than they were prepared to provide.[9] In any case, there was no integral role for the social work practitioner in the poverty program, for, in fact, the program itself was an organizational response to past social

---

[8] Cloward, Richard A. and Piven, Frances Fox, "We've Got Rights! The No-Longer Silent Welfare Poor," *The New Republic*, Aug. 5, 1967.

[9] Moynihan, Daniel P., *Maximum Feasible Misunderstanding*, Free Press, New York, 1969, p. 203.

failures that were often associated with social work's failures.

THE ASSOCIATION OF SOCIAL WORK PRACTICE WITH THE SOCIAL ILLS THAT AFFLICT SOCIETY

We have commented upon the affiliation of social work practice with social institutions, most particularly social work agencies, that has contributed to the lessening of regard for the effectiveness of the work of the practitioner. As social workers have not been very active in affecting questionable policies of the social agency network and indeed have participated in carrying them out, they cannot be held entirely innocent of the present-day consequences. Yet there are other factors that have contributed to the unfortunate state of affairs in which social work practice currently finds itself. Paramount among these is the necessary association of that practice with the most unpleasant problems confronting society.

There are several categories of misunderstanding that might help to explain the criticism of social work practice vis-à-vis the problems with which it deals.

On one level, social workers in the past have somewhat pretentiously made some promises they could not keep, such as when they said they could improve the condition of the poor through rehabilitative services offered in conjunction with money. This is probably one of the most vulnerable aspects of the long history of Social work practice. The social Darwinian concept that held the individual responsible for the economic condition of his life was the framework within which social work practice addressed the problem of poverty. Social workers were not alone in holding this view; it was the prevalent view of an early industrial society that found derivatives of Social Darwinism functional as a way to cope with poverty without affecting the economic system. The richest period of development of social casework methods occurred during the time that practitioners were attempting to strengthen the poor to cope with their lives. This direction of practice was undoubtedly a contributory factor to the restraint of government in addressing itself to the condition of poverty that was being created by the inequities of society and not by the characterological weaknesses of the person who was poor. In effect, the more successful the rehabilitative measures were in individual cases, the more it could be demonstrated that the person was capable of overcoming his poverty, and thus was basically responsible for having been poor, unemployed, and ill-housed.

In the present decade the civil rights thrust and a great deal of intellectual ferment have contributed to the potential demise of Social Darwinism. It is becoming clearer to society at last that the solution to poverty is a more equitable distribution of money; the solution to unemployment is jobs; the solution to illiteracy is education; and the solution to discrimination is equal opportunity. In no area of society's failure to provide for all citizens decent standards of living and working are social casework treatment or social services still expected to be effective or worthwhile. As an institution of society, social work has reflected the best and the worst movements of thought in that society; it can do no more. Perhaps in the present time, social work will be freed of its previously unclear commitment to cure or treat conditions of life that are not within its capacities to accomplish.

On another level, in those areas of social pathology that are not strictly subject to political or economic change, social work has been associated with problems of juvenile delinquency, illegitimacy, child abuse, family breakdown, mental illness, and the anomic effects of social and economic failure. It would be safe to say that there have been limited solutions forthcoming from the years of social work attention to these problems, and criticism of practice deficiencies in the arena of social work expertise is certainly no mere quibble. These failures may be ascribed partly to a severe lack of basic knowledge of causation and partly to systemic features of all the problems mentioned, where the multiplicity of causes have reached into all aspects of living and thus cannot be channeled by social work any more than by law, medicine, or education alone. It is somewhat paradoxical that in medicine the doctor is not held responsible for the diseases he does not yet understand, and the lawyer is not identified with increases in crime. Yet, social workers are often held accountable for psycho-social pathology that they do not yet understand or that are not amenable to any known methods. Nevertheless, it is obvious that there is need for massive efforts in basic social research in the field of social work. Typically, in the last decade when research became a popular tool in social work, it has been addressed to evaluation of methods and services and not primarily to basic causation of problems.[10]

On a third level, the fact of social work's association with the deprived people in our society may have also contributed to the criticism of the field. It is well known that lawyers do not like to have social work "bleeding hearts" on their juries, that the "do-goodism" of social workers is an epithet, and that the negative feelings of some citizens about minority groups, the poor, the sick, the disabled and the delinquent citizens in this country will be displaced on to social workers because they are in a field that is attempting to give service to deprived people. The person in trouble, be he client, tenant, patient, probationer, parolee or other consumer of social welfare services is generally the very person who is in difficulty with the society that provides the service, or is unable due to psycho-social reasons to cope by himself in society. Thus, social workers function in social agencies that are only tolerated by the larger society, in behalf of individuals who are viewed as

---

[10] As recent examples:

Beck, Dorothy Fahs, *Patterns in Use of Family Agency Service*, Family Service Association of America, New York, 1962.

Meyer, Henry, *et al.*, *Girls at Vocational High*, Russell Sage Foundation, New York, 1965.

State Communities Aid Association, *The Multi-Problem Dilemma*, Scarecrow Press, Metuchen, N.J., 1968.

not having made it, or as disadvantaged and thereby threatening to the normal order of life. The unpopularity of the cause of social work has been both its major value and the chief reason for its disparagement. No other profession can make this claim. The irony appears when social workers themselves succumb to this kind of criticism and find it to be of greater value to their self-esteem literally to leave the field of unpopular case problems and turn to those that will make them feel less downtrodden themselves.

Finally, there is an organizational level in which social work has been associated with the agency that might itself be the perpetrator of the social problem. For example, public housing may erect a functional but unappealing housing complex, set up strict rules of behavior for tenants, and devise stringent eligibility practices. When a social worker is hired to give social services to the tenants or to make the project community present fewer difficulties to the management, the social worker is asked to undo the effects of the management's self-imposed restrictions. He must help the tenants overcome the effects of the ugliness of the project, help them obey the rigid rules or plead for their revision, and ease the eligibility system by readying tenants to enter or by referring those who are excluded. The alternatives available to the practitioner in this typical situation of organizational self-defeat are very limited. He might refuse to work in the project; he might organize the tenants to rebel against discriminatory practices; or he might do the best he can to help the tenants cope with a dysfunctional housing system. As the practitioner pursues any of these courses of action, he will be subject to criticism by the housing management, the tenant, or the militant social reformer.

Another example of the organizational bind in which the well-meaning practitioner is often caught can be found in public assistance agencies. Legislation, budgetary limitations, and public attitudes combine to promote a dysfunctional program of income maintenance. Budgets are unmanageable, eligibility rules are exclusive, administrative policies are restrictive, and the total atmosphere reflects a philosophy of less-eligibility. Moreover, outside of the agency itself, inequities in society having to do with unfair income distribution, lack of job opportunities, and discrimination against already disadvantaged people create the necessity for public assistance as a residual and palliative social program. The social work practitioner then is expected to help clients adjust to the fundamental inequities in society as well as to the poor law provisions of the agency. Thus, the social worker becomes part of the inequitable system and subject to criticism on behalf of the system, even while he attempts to ameliorate its effect upon the people being served.

We have commented in this section about the plight of the social work practitioner who is associated with the ills of society and the dysfunctional systems created by society to cope with its problems. The social worker is in a position of being damned if he does and damned if he doesn't. It is in the nature of his work to be in such a position. His necessary association with the social work agency establishment and his lack of technical solutions to the problems the agencies seek to resolve will always subject him to criticism. The fact is that social work is a compensatory field of practice, as are many professional helping fields. Were the society going well, were people happy and comfortable, were there no illness and poverty and delinquency and social breakdown, there would be no need for social workers. Will the fine day ever come when they will be out of a job? It would appear unlikely that we are on the threshold of a utopian society; it would be fruitless to pursue the end of perfectability. The present imperfect urban society will probably continue to create its own limitations, and social workers—or some helping people—will continue to be called upon to help mitigate the severe psycho-social problems of society.

THE PULL BETWEEN THE AIMS OF PRACTICE
AND THOSE OF SOCIAL CHANGE

The inevitable question that must arise from our prior discussion is what is the use of it all? If social work practice cannot affect fundamentally the lives of the disadvantaged people in our society and if it must be integral to the establishment system itself, would it not be wiser to put the fervent energies of social work practitioners into the work of changing social institutions if not society itself? If, as we have noted, it is primarily society and not the individual that is responsible for the social problems in our world, why then would social work practice devote itself to individualization instead of the root cause of the difficulties?

Marris and Rein, whose book, *Dilemmas of Social Reform,* we referred to earlier, evaluated the early Community Action Program and assessed the reason for its failure to mobilize the poor in their own behalf and to make changes in social institutions. Marris and Rein say that:

> it seems unlikely that any program of community action so dependent upon a consensus of established leadership and public funds, could be at the same time an effective champion of radical democracy.[11]

The paradox seems evident now, that organized society will not be the source of support for forces that will overthrow it. While the early reformers in CAP, such as Mobilization for Youth, experimented with circumventing the rigid bureaucracies, they, too, had to devise administrative procedures and controls. Furthermore, since they were without political support, the confrontations they risked ultimately were doomed, and once again the poor were offered promises that could not be kept. Moynihan has commented upon the fact that the initiative for the anti-poverty program came not from the poor or from political pressures, but rather from technical knowledge and professional concerns.[12] Marris and Rein have questioned whether it is ever possible for a sophisticated professional staff to work out programs in equal partnership with the people they serve.[13]

---

[11] Marris and Rein, *Op. cit.*, p. 183.

[12] Moynihan, Daniel P., "Professionalization of Reform," *The Public Interest,* Fall 1965, pp. 6–16.

[13] Marris and Rein, *Op. cit.*, p. 185.

We see in these comments on the poverty program the massive effort by government and foundations to effect social change on an institutional level, the dilemmas to which we have referred earlier. The first problem is that radical change desired by the lower class cannot be effected in social structures without political power that usually can be attained only through the vote or through peaceful or violent protest. The second problem is that probably due to the vast affluence of the middle class in this country and the pressures upon the total population to strive for this affluence and its symbols as well as its comforts, it does not seem that either the vote or revolution will evoke strong popular or political middle-class support in the program of basic social reorganization. The third problem is, given the above two issues, professional social workers, doctors, lawyers, and teachers will probably continue to be the major instigators of incipient change, the ones who bring conditions to the public's awareness, the ones who will on occasion join with their client and patient and student groups as they make their grass-roots statements aloud, and the ones who will try *in the meantime* to assuage the unfortunate effects of the health, education, legal, and welfare institutions in this country.

It is difficult to imagine how professionals, even an army of them, could achieve the power to effect basic social change through their separate technical expertness. The most that they will be able to effect will be a middle range kind of change and surely an evolutionary one. Such a statement might be a disappointment to the activist student, professional or militant, but it is very important to our discussion of social work practice to differentiate between *acknowledgement* of economic social inequities in this country and *possibilities* for action in a professional role. The professional social worker performing a residual function and helping to ameliorate the gross inequities of the social system may indeed contribute to the continuance of that system. But in the course of this, people may be helped to live more comfortably, and this aim of practice is a choice that must be made in a value context, as well as in face of the realities of political life.

Richard A. Cloward, a long-time and persistent critic of the role of social work in society, has said that:

> social reforms seek to humanize systems without acknowledging, much less challenging, the fundamental inequalities upon which these systems are based.[14]

Cloward is not prepared

> to identify the rationality of the technician with the common good . . . or the use of political subdivisions to maintain social and economic inequalities.

He, along with students representative of the New Left continually ask the same question: Can social progress come about without basic change in social institutions?

In order to answer this question, one would need to define the degree of social change being proposed and the kinds of realignments in political and economic power for which one would settle. A complete and radical rearrangement of social forces in this country might be a value for which all progressive-minded people might strive; indeed, such a revolution in our social structure may be inevitable for all we know. Cloward unquestionably presents a compelling argument, particularly when one views inadequate and degrading programs like public assistance, for one must ask how such a social device can be humanized or improved, when its basic purposes are so intertwined with an economy that supports economic class differences, and, therefore, relies upon public assistance programs to supplement the income of the poor. Cloward is right in suggesting that the more improvements that are made in an unjust system, the more subtle are the means for making the injustice palatable. This issue can be seen in most public institutions which are structured for the poor especially in

---

[14] Cloward, Richard A., in *Social Theory and Social Invention,* Herman Stein, ed., Case Western Reserve Press, Cleveland, Ohio, 1968, "Commentary on a Subversive Version of the Great Society," pp. 70–74.

order to compensate for the inequalities promoted by the total American economic system. Cloward asks if social workers are prepared to participate in this form of compensation, when they might better support the forces of revolutionary change in the total system.

It has been forty years since Porter R. Lee raised the question about social work being addressed to cause or function,[15] and the field has yet to lay to rest this dichotomy. Social work has both cause and function, complementarily and integrally, but the matter of social change is a nagging and complex one when it is viewed as the aim of social work *practice*. Social work itself is so much a reflection of society that it, of all of the fields of service, may be in the least strategic position to change it. Presently, social workers function under public and voluntary auspices that are themselves the power structure often intent upon maintaining society as it is. This is but one of the political binds in which social work finds itself, but social change has many meanings, and the scope of change can vary and range from institutional to individual change. In the middle range there are also levels of revolutionary and evolutionary change that would have significance.

In the first quarter of this century when the transition from a rural to an industrialized society was in process, the inevitable social ills of child labor, outdoor poor relief and the explicit translation of the Elizabethan Poor Law, and exploitation of the worker and the poor were paramount concerns to early social workers. In this "cause" phase of social work, charismatic and highly individualistic social reformers literally stormed the barricades to bring to public and official attention the harrowing scope of social injustice.[16] By the 1940s when the Depression had led to enormous organizational reforms, the old charitable, benevolent

---

[15] Lee, Porter R., "Social Work . . . Cause or Function?," Presidential Address at National Conference of Social Work, 1929.

[16] Examples of early reformers in social work were: Edith Abbott, Grace Abbott, Jane Addams, Sophinisba P. Breckenridge, Edward T. Devine, Florence Kelley, Julia Lathrope, Josephine Shaw Lowell, Lillian D. Wald, and Amos G. Warner.

voices that sought social change were themselves transformed into administrative channels, and the unique expres-
siveness of the reformer was obscured by the constraints
placed upon him by the official chair he occupied. However,
today we still hear the cry, "where is the social reformer of
yesterday?" Of course, he is gone, or more explicitly he has
taken the leadership of a vast social welfare bureaucracy.
Once in a while he serves as a representative of professional
social work to plead a just social cause to the Congress, but,
again, in a depersonalized role as an interpreter of issues
and not as a personal leader. Occasionally, we find the social
reformer of our day as magazine writer or panelist on radio
and television shows, and through these media he must
compete with the uncounted other demands upon the eyes,
ears, and passions of the multi-media-ed public. Finally, we
see the social reformer in politics, not often elected, but
often provided with a platform on the dais or at the parade.
Whatever mold the social reformer as a personality has had
in the past, his personal influence today has decreased, and
he has been replaced by institutionalized programs of reform and the ideologies of reform that are expressed most
virulently in university settings. Social reform is still vital
as a necessary check upon democratic conservatism; it is
only that the voices of social reform seem to have become
institutionalized.

What of the role of social work practice in social reform
—or social change, as we now call it? There are a range of
positions that can be taken about this matter. We can view
social change roughly on three levels, not all of which are
compatible, even though proponents of different modes of
change might view social problems in the same way. We
can assume that there would be some agreement that our
social institutions, mainly those of the health, education
and welfare complex, are sometimes dysfunctional for this
urban and technical age. One mode of change would address the basic institutions themselves, and its adherents
would seek to rearrange the structures, roots of power and
perhaps the auspices of these institutions, so as to free

them from outworn bureaucratic strictures, class affiliations, and political positions. An example might be found in the change of public assistance to social insurance programs to provide for more equitable income maintenance on a massive scale. Perhaps even before this, one might propose more radical measures to redistribute income in the country, but it would be safe to say that the fate of any such proposals for fundamental economic change in this country appropriately rest in the political rather than in the social work practice arena. Another example would be the whole matter of housing, where social change would occur through urban redevelopment, rather than through piecemeal housing arrangements that have proved to be so inadequate. The level of social change sought here would be basic to the institutions themselves, for it would be understood that those institutions are to a large degree responsible for the troubles people have in getting help from them.

On the other extreme, where the same assumptions may exist about the causes of dysfunctional health, education, and welfare institutions, social change as a concept would not be addressed at all to the institutions themselves but rather to the individual in an effort to strengthen him to cope with the personal effects of institutional lacks. Proponents of this approach may feel inadequately prepared to cope with fundamental attacks upon society, or may actually hold still to the Social Darwinian belief that it is the individual's lacks that inhibit him from overcoming the institution's shortcomings.

Criticisms about social work practice usually come from the first mentioned school of thought that adheres to the aim of basic social change, and often the quality of that practice is not even at issue. Rather, as in Cloward's position, criticism is based upon the *fact* of practice, particularly good practice and the role it plays in obfuscating the real issues which are plaguing this society. The polarity of these positions about social change reflects the dilemma for every social work practitioner of social conscience, just as the lack of a cure for cancer must affect every general medical practitioner, as every overcrowded school must affect every good teacher and as every strike of a civil service staff must affect a socially conscious mayor. Indeed, it is very hard to argue that, *given equal alternatives,* social workers ought to refine their practices so that people can be helped to survive the inequities in our society, rather than that they ought to address all of their expertise to a thoroughgoing change or revolution of society itself. Yet, the hard fact is that there are no equal alternatives, and that this country is probably not on the brink of a revolution at this present moment. It seems increasingly unlikely that a total and systematic change is going to occur in our society at this point in time. Moreover, if such a radical movement were to occur, it would undoubtedly be more effectively carried out by the aroused masses of the poor, the black community, and youth, than by social workers in their roles as practitioners. Marris and Rein state the case best when they argue that

> any approach to reform must accept some practical limit to its aims of work within a setting that partly frustrates its ideals. But by ignoring the wider issue . . . risk deceiving both themselves and others as to what they could achieve, and provoke a corresponding disillusionment.[17]

We have still to mention that middle level of social change, the aims of which may include focus upon both the individual and the institution in an effort to improve the conditions of life in this imperfect society. It seems to us circular reasoning to state that a practice of any kind is irrelevant while the conditions persist that require that practice. Who can deny the presence of inequity in our society? Social work practitioners must affirm it and, as *practitioners* devote themselves to ways of mitigating the conditions, as well as the effects upon people. The position taken by this book is that the social work practitioner must recognize the issues—both the social problems and the criticisms about social work failures to act—and then take action through practice measures to deal with institutional

[17] Marris and Rein, *Op. cit.,* p. 91.

dysfunction and with the people who need the services of these institutions. The constraints on practice are manifold, the problems are immense, and our practice tools have only moderate scope. Yet, practice we must, or surrender to passive acceptance of the inevitable turmoil.

Reviewing what we have stated so far, it seems that social work as a practice has suffered more than slings and arrows in the last thirty years. Social workers have been associated with and thus indirectly accused of creating or abetting the social problems with which they have tried to cope; they have been part of the conservative establishment of social welfare and thus have been subject to the just and unjust criticisms expressed by the public that maintains the conservative structure, by the client who is not served by it, and by the social scientist who wants it changed. Furthermore, social workers, representing the range of critiques, have taken off after themselves in their professional literature, often pleading guilty to inaction, and always questioning the purpose of it all. And Gilbert and Sullivan talked about the policeman's lot!

THE DRIVE TOWARD PROFESSIONALIZATION
AND SPECIALIZATION

Since Abraham Flexner in 1915 asked the question "Is Social Work A Profession?,"[18] many social workers have sought to demonstrate that it was, while others restrained themselves from a professional commitment or didn't care. The drive toward professionalism is understandable in a technical society where status does indeed come from the symbols and trappings of expertise, if not its substantive content; it becomes a matter of self-preservation for practitioners in all fields of public service to draw their own circles within which no outsider may enter. Social workers particularly, who have traditionally worked in host agencies where the primary service is medi-

---

[18] Flexner, Abraham, "Is Social Work A Profession?" National Conference of Social Work, 1915.

cine, psychiatry, law, and institutional care, have felt the need to announce themselves as professionals. The whole society is becoming more specialized in the services it provides and social workers are only as human as every one else.

The critical issues about the state of social work practice do not derive only from the drive toward professionalism but rather from the preoccupation with it. The hallmark of professionalism is the guarantee of service and protection to the public, and we would surely not quarrel with this aim. But when licensing, registration, or certification tend to restrict services in an era when masses of personnel are needed then the aim of public service becomes displaced. A second characteristic of professionalism is the presence of specialized knowledge, a theory of practice and of the object of practice that is exclusive to the particular professional pursuit. Again, we would acclaim the presence of such knowledge, for it would enrich the practice of social work and thus the services provided to people. But one of the facts about social work is that it is a borrower of knowledge from social and behavioral sciences; it does not ordinarily embark on basic research; instead it puts together this borrowed knowledge in very particular ways for very particular uses. The way in which social work utilizes basic knowledge of human behavior and social systems is what gives social work its stamp. The critical issue here is not whether or not social work has discovered its own secrets but rather that it may be spending too much effort on presenting itself as a profession, when, in fact, it may not be so important that it be one at all. The very suspicion that it may not be a profession, or if it is, that it is a "new" one, tends to make social workers somewhat defensive and overreactive to incursion by others; thus it turns inward and "tools up." This trend may account in part for the sense of alienation felt by the community that perceives social workers as passing them by.

The question of social work expertise and special knowledge is a complicated one. Many professions have carved out pieces of life to which they address their skills, even though the boundaries of their expertise may at times have seemed blurred. For example, whatever the likenesses between the doctor and the nurse, the physicist and the biologist or the chemist, the lawyer and the diplomat, there is seldom question about the basic identity of the professional practitioner in question. He has the reputation for at least having knowledge about very particular aspects of life and what to do about them. What is the knowledge arena in which the social work practitioner functions?

It is said that the boundaries of social work practice could encompass all of society, the whole individual, the range of conditions from health to pathology, and a very large repertoire of skills addressed to improved individual coping, institutional change, social policy and planning, and the list grows longer as social workers become part of new social inventions. In effect, it would seem that there are hardly any boundaries to the knowledge that is necessary for social workers to have just in order to get through a working day. Whereas other professional specialists become expert by narrowing their knowledge parameters, social workers must expand beyond measure to broaden horizons of knowledge. Furthermore, the difference between "hard" and "soft" knowledge is more real than apparent when one compares the biologist's laboratory with the social worker's community or agency as the focus of his action. Social workers deal with unknown and perhaps unknowable complexities in human life; the causes of human stress are multiple and their etiology cannot always be discovered. The kind, scope, and depth of knowledge sought for and needed in social work practice makes imperative the borrowing we have mentioned, and differentiates the social worker from other professional practitioners. In a way the clergyman could be perceived similarly. He is accountable to society for values that belong to everyone, concerned as he is with the total human condition, as well as for interpretation of metaphysical spheres. But unlike the social worker, the clergyman is not asked to prove that his methods work, nor is he expected to solve the unknowns like the after-life which are related to his area of competence.

Specialization in social work was inevitable, for it would be impossible for a single practitioner to become expert in the extensive range of problems and the methods devised to resolve them. However, the specialization fervor created a kind of parochialism that may have interfered with sound practice after all. At present, social work is organized or departmentalized in several ways, some of which intersect and overlap others.

Fields of practice as a concept[19] has actually grown up with the entire field of social work. Thus previously social workers identified such fields as family service, child welfare, psychiatric social work, medical social work, corrections, and school social work. These defined fields of practice derived specifically from the settings in which social work traditionally had been carried on. In an effort to move away from the mark of apprenticeship and to provide for generic education and practice which would not be colored entirely by the specific setting, the concept of fields of practice at least made provision for the practitioner to become expert in a larger arena than a particular agency; he could move within his general field as a specialist in child welfare, family welfare, etc. This approach to the concept of fields of practice gave social work trouble, however, because it was unnecessarily restrictive in an era when nonspecified settings and fields were opening up new vistas of service, for example, community psychiatry, labor

[19] Bartlett, Harriet, *Analyzing Social Work Practice By Fields*, National Association of Social Workers, New York, 1961.

Kahn, Alfred J., "Social Work Fields of Practice," in *Encyclopedia of Social Work*, National Association of Social Workers, New York, 1965, pp. 750–754.

N.A.S.W. Commission on Social Work Practice, Sub-Committee on Fields of Practice, "Identifying Fields of Practice in Social Work," *Social Work*, Vol. V, No. 2, April 1962, pp. 7–8.

Studt, Eliot, "Organizing Resources for More Effective Practice," *Trends in Social Work Practice and Knowledge*, 10th Anniversary Symposium, N.A.S.W., New York, 1966, pp. 41–54.

unions, civil rights organizations, client organizations, housing complexes, and as yet unspecified social utilities and developmental services. The field could not expand its scope by continually adding on new kinds of settings; sooner or later the definitions of where practice was to occur had to be reconceptualized. Another reason for the restrictions involved in the fields of practice concept was that the single-purpose agency or the single-function field had become dysfunctional for our times. The mobility of the population, the view of the systemic interrelatedness of all aspects of people's lives and the multiplicity of causation for all psycho-social problems made it difficult to perceive the psycho-social situation divisible into fields that were once convenient for organizational purposes but not necessarily for the people being served.

It is common that when a client goes into a single-function agency, he tends to define his problem, or it is defined for him, in accordance with the function of that agency. Thus, if he has a marital problem and his child somehow gets caught in the middle of his struggle with his wife, a man who goes to a child welfare agency may erroneously view placement of his child as a solution to his situation. The traditional division into fields of practice undoubtedly contributed to the critical state of social work practice, because the concept did not follow the natural life style of people in trouble, and it forced upon its clientele a mold that was originally best suited to a practice that was attempting to professionalize itself.

> A fields emphasis leads to an orientation more to process than to task, since participants in a field become preoccupied with the issue of their distinctiveness, emphasize it in all phases of their work and tend to be satisfied if the distinctiveness is refined and adequately manifested.[20]

More recently, in 1963 the National Association of Social Workers agreed upon more broadly defined councils (of specific interest), such as social work in schools, medical

[20] Kahn, *Op. cit.*, p. 751.

and health services, mental health and psychiatric services, correctional services, family and children's services, group services, community planning and development, and councils on social work research and on social work administration. The intent of these subdivisions was that they be flexible and not misconstrued as areas of competence. The current situation remains in flux, but it is evident that any structure that would account for specialized interest must follow closely the current conceptualizations of practice and must hold out promise of rich substantive knowledge in whatever definition or organization of "field" that finally is devised.

Another kind of specialization that has derived out of the unformed matrix of social work practice has been that confined to methodology. Thus, where fields of practice would remain a constant factor, casework, group work, community organization, administration, staff development, and research are the variables that describe the social work method specialities. We will deal differently here with the first three methods, because it is evident that the last three would be applicable to all fields of practice or all arenas in which social work practice is carried on.

The defined practice methods of *social casework, group work,* and *community organization* have all evolved unevenly. Considering the range of times covered by the development of each of the methods, it would be a major historical achievement to draw clarifying comparisons among them. Each has taken its own route through history, having been concerned with its particular unit of attention, all having been influenced by their own reference groups, favorite knowledges, and specific subcultures. It is not the aim of this book to trace the histories of the separate methods, nor to evaluate the impact upon human life of one or all of them. We shall come upon the scene only in the present, when the concerns and sometimes the techniques of the three methodologies *appear* to have converged. The lack of agreement in the field of social work as to viewing the three methods in a unified way has created much confusion for all concerned—students, clients, practitioners who see so much that they hold in common, but must call to each other over such vast historical and theoretical distances. It would seem that a holistic view of man in society would not rely on disparate views of him as an individual, in a group, or as a member of a number of communities. Despite the fact that all three methods share similar professional values and certain areas of knowledge and that all three comprise the practice of social work, presently there are real and imagined jurisdictional disputes that make it difficult to combine the methods into one significant practice. Of course the higher the level of abstraction, the closer one can get to agreement, but we must be careful to avoid the scylla of reductionism while staying out of the way of the charybdis of separatism. It would be as wrong to prematurely melt down into one mold the three different methods as it would be to maintain their different directions for the sake of the territorial imperative alone. Nor is it simply a matter of going back to the drawing board, because the three methods have by now become institutionalized and therefore meet certain latent as well as overt functions for their practitioners.

There have been efforts in recent years to bring together the three methods in social work education,[21] where students are taught from the beginning that they are "generic" practitioners, and they utilize knowledge and skills that indeed suggest that this long-sought-for integration has been accomplished. Other educational efforts have addressed each method separately and have attempted to broaden the repertoire of skills and techniques. Thus, rather than approaching the problem from the point of view of a basic integration of casework, group work, and community organization, the second view has suggested that techniques could be borrowed and utilized easily within the expanded primary method with which the student or practitioner is identified.

---

[21] Briar, Scott, "Flexibility and Specialization in Social Work Education," *Social Work Education Reporter,* December 1968.

It is indeed unfortunate that territorial imperatives have thus far postponed a solution to this serious practice dilemma. It is obvious that the nature of the social problem being addressed should determine the kind of method used, but it is a present fact that each method in social work views its work with individuals, groups and communities as being within its own sphere of competence. There are many good historical reasons for the compartmentalization of the three methods, some having to do with the political and economic developments of the eras in which each speciality became connected with organized social work, for each approach was intended to serve a particular function for society. These functions have changed as society has changed. Also, the expansion of knowledge has made it impossible for professional practitioners in all fields to become experts in everything attended to by his particular profession. The world is very complicated, and no one can know everything.

This writer, after several excursions in a number of directions, has made a stop at various stations, once seeking basic integration into a unitary practice, and at another time seeing the answer in an enlarged scope for each practice method.[22] The dilemma is not resolved at this writing, and yet the complicated threads of social work practice must be unravelled so that clients may be served. It seems that the only way for a caseworker responsibly to discuss practice at the present time is within the social casework framework. It is this stance that is taken in this book, presented with full awareness that the methods of community organization and group work each will address its own unit of attention with its own unique approach. The view of practice held by this writer is an expanded view of social casework, which has been committed for fifty years to addressing the person-in-situation context. Where the boun-

[22] Meyer, Carol H., "The Changing Concept of Individualized Services," *Social Casework*, May 1966.

Meyer, Carol H., "Integrating Practice Demands in Social Work Education," *Social Casework*, Dec. 1968.

daries of this unit of attention converge upon the boundaries devised by the other social work methods, this will be a source of elation. We seek the final aim of permeation of all methodological boundaries so that the field of social work ultimately will claim a unitary practice, with specializations restricted to substantive areas and not to method ideologies. If the presentation of this practice model can be entertained by community organization, group work, and social casework, this caseworker will gladly surrender the casework appellation in favor of the combined, socially instrumental concept of social work practice.

> Maybe the way to go about identifying social work practice activities is not within the traditional boundaries of casework, group work and community work at all, but across lines, by asking ourselves what kinds of problems call for what kinds of services and actions. It is possible that the ways we perceive a situation, define it, and go about treating it are shaped a priori by the particular methods in which we have allegiance or in which we have skill.[23]

Because the field of social work is not yet prepared to relate method to problem, we are presently forced to straddle two notions at once, to talk simultaneously about the role of the social caseworker and the role of the social work practitioner. As a partial resolution to this dilemma, this book will address social casework as a methodological field, but mainly it will call the practitioner a social worker instead of a social caseworker. Be this teasing on the part of the author, or merely a symptom of gross fantasizing, we seek to demonstrate the validity of the concept of the wish-fulfilling prophecy.

Professional practice is defined by its responsiveness to society's expression of need for particular services that a profession is able to provide. Professional social work practice, including its major methods of casework, group work,

---

[23] Perlman, Helen Harris, "Social Work Methods: A Review of the Past Decade," *Trends in Social Work Practice and Knowledge*, Vol. 10, Anniversary Symposium N.A.S.W., New York, 1966, pp. 94–95.

and community organization have accumulated techniques to cope with certain specified requirements of society. Furthermore, social-work values are quite up-to-date, in that they explicitly observe the dignity of individual man and his right to self-determination and self-fulfillment. Traditional principles used in social work have also worn well in this new participatory society, where manipulating social resources on behalf of the client and serving as advocate are most important among these principles. Social work, perhaps more than any other field of endeavor, has served at the expressed behest of organized society through its social agencies and social services in hospitals, clinics, courts, schools, and institutions. It is a field that has had a great deal of experience in being a practice arm of society's prevalent values.

Yet, despite its apparent utilitarian functions, as a field it is in a critical state due in large measure to its integral connections with the unplanned society in which we live; as society has developed haltingly in the United States, so has social work. At present the world in turmoil provides mixed messages to social work practice, which is itself in a tumultuous state. Its aims need to be articulated and its sights need to be turned outward, away from concern for its own well-being.

2

social casework . . . along the route of history

No longer a sedative for social revolution, nor a shock-absorber for the unmerited blows of an unkind economic fate, social work can become a catalyst, bent on releasing human potentialities.

——Kathleen Woodroofe[24]

---

[24] Woodroofe, *Op. cit.*, p. 227.

IN THE PREVIOUS CHAPTER we have commented upon the critical state of social work practice, assuming that the social context and the aims of practice are by far the most significant factors that have contributed to the present state of social work in the urban scene. It would not be sufficient to hold up the methods and techniques of practice by themselves as the cause of all of the difficulties, just as it would not be sufficient to improve and refine those methods and suggest that everything then would be all right. It will be a continuing theme in this book that it is the uses to which methods are put that really define their effectiveness in society. Perhaps it has been the reliance on technique without reference to its purposes that has been the most serious handicap to the modernization of social work practice. We have observed in Chapter I that the social policy framework and organization of agencies within which social workers have worked with their clients over the last half a century have influenced the goals and methods of practice, just as have the attention to specialization and professionalization. Methods and techniques, after all, are only tools or expressions of the practitioner's commitment to particular aims.

An analogy to medicine might be useful here. When a surgical technique is refined in medicine, it does not stand by itself as a solution to a disease. Its place in the range of medical procedures has to be allocated. As surgery is a radical process, in order to assess the values of the procedure, the patient must have available to him some prior medical and less radical solutions to his problems, and he must be assured that postoperative care will be so effective that he will not die from surgery. Placing the procedure in a socio-economic context, the surgical technique would be rather meaningless if it were so expensive that it could not be placed at the disposal of the general public and find broad social usefulness. Thus, the procedure itself might be an extravagant miracle of surgery and yet it would be socially impractical or meaningless. Analogously and particularly in social work, all techniques need to be evaluated in a similar way in order to assess their relevancy.

Later we will discuss the updating of practice in social casework as an individualizing practice in the urban society, but at this juncture it is important to comment upon some of the developments that have contributed to the critical state of this field of social work practice. Social casework has not been alone among social work methods in its accumulation of problems, but it has had the longest tradition in both theory and practice of social work, so it has naturally had the longest time in which to make mistakes as well as to make a contribution to methodology. The very criticisms of social casework that have questioned its preoccupation with technique, treatment, and over-specialization in regard to the individual client may here be turned to our advantage in this discussion. For the long history of social casework has reflected the social and economic development of this country, as well as the knowledge extant in any particular area. Through examining the past practices of social casework, we may come upon insights about modes of individualizing help, some of which have proved to be dysfunctional over time, whereas others may yet prove to have continuing validity.

In order not to exposit a descriptive history of social casework, which has been dealt with in other places,[25] it might serve our critical purposes best if we examine themes in the development of casework through an urban lens. We will be able to adjudge the directions taken by this method, not according to their functional value at the time they evolved, but rather according to their validity in present-day terms. In other words, although history may justify most actions, we are not interested here in justifications, but in

---

[25] Becker, Dorothy G., "Early Adventures in Social Casework: The Charity Agent, 1880–1910," *Social Casework*, May 1963, pp. 255–261.

Garton, Nina R. and Otto, Herbert A., *The Development of Theory and Practice in Social Casework*, Chas. C. Thomas, Springfield, Ill., 1964.

Hellenbrand, Shirley C., "Main Currents in Social Casework, 1918–1936," (Unpub.) Doctoral Dissertation, Columbia University School of Social Work, 1965.

Reynolds, Bertha C., *An Unchartered Journey: 50 Years of Growth in Social Work*, Citadel Press, New York, 1963.

sorting out from a network of often conflicting themes, those that would serve today as functional and relevant in an individualizing social work practice in the urban world. In order to make the evaluation of the casework method as objective as possible, it will be helpful to use some criteria against which past approaches can be assessed for their current usefulness. Naturally, the criteria selected would need to rely upon certain assumptions about the inevitable role of practice in today's world. Simply as a matter of organization, these assumptions are fully drawn in Chapters 4 and 5, where we present a view of the urban scene and social work's part in it. At this time, in the context of discussing the critical state of social work practice, we ask the reader to take those assumptions for granted (or turn first to those chapters) as the basis for the following criteria.

In the assessment of the continuing validity of certain past practices or themes in social casework, we would want to judge:

1. Does it continue to justify the promise it held out?
2. Does it provide, as an open system, for new knowledge, new uses, and new adaptations to social conditions?
3. Is it applicable to large segments of the urban population in a developmental rather than residual organization of social work services?

In a sense, although we will be looking at some of the "wrong turns" taken in social casework, it must be understood that in retrospect it is not hard to know better what "might have been," and it is not possible to view a turn in any direction out of its historical context. We will look at *old themes* that were once functional for their times but may *no longer be useful*. Then we will view those themes that are old but might have *new uses*. Some ideas are viable and are not tied to outworn aims, and we will not reject them merely because they are traditional. This "review" of themes in social casework will serve as background to our later discussion of new themes and a new model for social work practice in the modern urban society.

There is a growing literature about the contribution of Mary Richmond as the original theorist of social casework.[26] Whether we view her today, in our view erroneously, as "something of an embarrassment to professional social work"[27] or as a scholar who attempted to make a transition from the post-Victorian morality to the industrial age of science, it would be impossible to deny the fact that Miss Richmond did, indeed, codify the instrumentality that came to be known as social diagnosis and the core of diagnostic social casework. Although it is undeniable that her major work, *Social Diagnosis*,[28] is in today's lights an exhaustive model for practice, it did follow the inventory models of the period and it was the first and the most notable effort to translate good neighborliness into a methodology. This is not the place to ponder whether such a translation should have occurred at all, for as Lubove points out, "early efforts to differentiate clients were frequently undermined by the paternalistic moralism characteristic of 19th century philanthropy and by the lack of any science of human behavior."[29] Thus Richmond's contribution was to demonstrate causation in the environment through scientific means and to overcome in this way the tendency to view the person as morally responsible for his plight. Her view of social diagnosis was

> the attempt to make as exact a definition as possible of the situation and personality of a human being in some social need—of his situation and personality, that is, in relation to the other human beings upon whom he in any way

---

[26] Pumphrey, Muriel, "Mary Richmond and the Rise of Professional Social Work in Baltimore: The Foundation of a Creative Career," (Unpub.) Doctoral Dissertation, Columbia University School of Social Work, 1956.

Social Casework (Entire Issue) October 1961, "100th Anniversary of Mary E. Richmond's Birth."

[27] Berleman, William C., "Mary Richmond's *Social Diagnosis* in Retrospect," *Social Casework*, July 1968, pp. 395–402.

[28] Richmond, Mary E., *Social Diagnosis*, Russell Sage, New York, 1917.

[29] Lubove, *Op. cit.*, p. 23.

depends or who depend upon him, and in relation to the social institutions in his community.[30]

Were there ever in history a direct route taken from the past to the present, this definition of social diagnosis might serve as the immediate precursor to a modern view of individualizing social work practice.

The intervening eras between 1917, when *Social Diagnosis* was published, and the present day reflected the knowledge and commitments that were extant in each period. Thus, in the 1920s the postwar disillusionment set in and the times were characterized by introspective rather than social preoccupations. In social work, the Mental Hygiene movement and the prevalent interest in rehabilitation and psychiatry as it evolved out of World War I directed social workers on a course that turned out to be a detour from the one set by Richmond. In the 1930s the Depression had so vast an impact upon the country that the relief function was taken over by Government. Social caseworkers were in a sense left with no other access to the client group besides one that would effectively address the personality. As this was the period when Freudian theory found its way into the mainstream of intellectual life in America, it served to support the growing attention in social casework upon personality. The 1940s of course provided a deterrent through World War II, with its emphasis upon the adaptations of soldiers to the condition of war, and the 1950s appeared to social workers as to most Americans as a period of postwar abundance that provided little active impetus to address the inequities in society. The person-in-situation and incipient institutional theoretical approach devised by Richmond, despite the significant influences of Gordon Hamilton, Bertha Reynolds, and Fern Lowry, had to wait about fifty years before it was again to find relevance in a revised conceptualization of social casework.

Recalling that industrialization as a social invention was not being universally recognized as a *condition* that was

---

[30] Richmond, *Op. cit.*, p. 363.

beyond the control of individuals, we can understand the probable intentions of the caseworkers in the 1920s as they sought individual solutions to social problems. Nevertheless, in accordance with our criteria, the direction taken by early social caseworkers was a "wrong turn" in the sense that it held out greater promise than it was able to justify; casework with individuals did not resolve either individual or social problems. Nor did the developing theory and practice provide in the 1920s for an approach that would be addressed to social conditions. Thus we might question the openness of the theoretical system at that time. Furthermore, social casework came out of a charitable era and its practitioners devoted themselves to the poor primarily; it was not a practice that was being made applicable to all people, and it couldn't have been, where the helping people were all of one class and the clients being helped were of another. As social casework evolved from the philanthropic movement, it was propelled from the beginning into a continuing identification with the techniques of working with the poor.[31]

It is a bit tricky in these days of rediscovery of the poor and heightened criticism of social casework for having left the poor in its search for technical expertise, to question this past methodological affiliation with the poor alone. Actually, these were clientele whose primary problems derived from the inequitable social system which was not amenable to casework methods. But we have noted some of the ways in which the use of casework may have contributed to the long silent social response to the conditions of poverty. The ambivalence about the client group that was to be the focus of casework attention remained to plague caseworkers for years; they have been guilty when they have not worked with the poor, and ineffective in ameliorating the conditions of the poor. It would appear that an individually centered practice cannot be conceptualized around a class of people, for poverty as a social-economic-

---

[31] *Social Casework* (Entire issue) "Who Spoke for the Poor?" 1880–1914," Feb. 1968.

political condition must be dealt with by appropriate social-economic-political strategies.[32] Social casework was caught in the bind of developing a general individualizing theory of practice out of specialized and inappropriate concentration upon only certain poor individuals. This may explain why part of the responsibility for the failure in the field of poverty was assigned to social casework. We are not saying that casework should have abandoned work with the poor; rather, we are only suggesting that provision of services to the poor became hopelessly confused with an unfortunate theoretical justification of the conditions of poor people. When social conditions serve to advance a theory, it is dangerous business. In the laboratory it is a familiar mode of theory development to work with guinea pigs and white mice. However, in social work, society brought together the practitioner and the poor client and it might have been an unfortunate alliance. Practitioners developed practice and policy biases, and the poor were promised a good deal more than could ever have been delivered. From this viewpoint, perhaps the first wrong turn was that Mary Richmond translated neighborliness into professionalism. Perhaps the poor would have been better served by their neighbors who would have had no pretense toward improving their social condition.

It is popular to decry the wrong turn inward that was made by social casework in the 1920s, when the impact of Freud's theories was beginning to be felt in this country. Again, history is its own judge, and as we look back to the early days of casework practice it is understandable that the search for a dynamic theory of human behavior seemed to be rewarded in the presence of psychoanalytic theory. Although there have been modifications of the original theory, it remains even today as a coherent and extremely useful theory. Social workers over the years have come to rely on other theoretical formulations, such as those developed by Rank and more recently those that refer back again

[32] Meyer, Carol H., "Casework Below the Poverty Line," *Social Work Practice*, Columbia University Press, New York, 1965, pp. 229–242.

to behaviorist conceptions. Obviously there is no single theoretical explanation for human behavior, and one must therefore rely upon the characteristics of a "good theory" in order to evaluate it.[33] Freudian psychoanalytic theory seems to meet these criteria, and it has been useful for social casework to be able to borrow from this knowledge. The "wrong turn" was not that caseworkers became preoccupied with the knowing of the theory; the error was in their attempt to apply it as a practice. Perhaps it was necessary to translate literally into practice the concepts that were so startling to the intellect; in any event, that is what happened in social casework practice. Caseworkers spent a good many years, certainly through the 1930s, 1940s, and 1950s, "tooling up" and refining their method to conform with the popular psychoanalytic theory. Perhaps this was a reflection of a general trend in society that was turning "inward." In the long view it was not an unimportant quest, for any method of working with people would need a theory of people, and this was a profound theory with tremendous and valuable influence upon the individualizing method of casework.[34]

What has become one of the sorest issues in the criticisms of social casework has been the attention paid to intra-psychic functions which preoccupied caseworkers for

---

[33] Whiteman, Martin, "A Conceptualization of Freudian Psychology," (Mimeo) Presented at The Annual Workshop for Faculty and Field Instructors at the Columbia University School of Social Work, March 27, 1967.

The following criteria of a "good" scientific theory were stated as: 1. *Range* or scope, the extensiveness of the phenomena explained; 2. *Economy* or parsimony, restriction of the number of concepts to less than the behaviors the theory is called upon to explain; 3. *Testability,* or application of the theory in other contexts outside of the testing situation.

Freudian theory reaches toward the aim of attempting to explain as many phenomena as possible with the fewest number of assumptions.

[34] Hamilton, Gordon, "A Theory of Personality, Freud's Contribution to Social Work," *Ego Psychology and Dynamic Casework,* Howard J. Parad, ed., Family Service Association of America, New York, 1958, pp. 11–37.

a long time and postponed their grappling with the external, social side of life. Yet in looking back we can see that there were limited alternatives, as it was not possible to affect social change through a practice methodology, and the very coherence of the psychoanalytical theory of human behavior held out great intellectual attraction. The social sciences had not offered the same organized, internally consistent set of ideas, and fragmented concepts about society were hardly as useful as a total theory of human development and behavior. It is important to recall the state of knowledge in the social sciences thirty and forty years ago, when sociology was largely descriptive and not dynamic as it is now and as Freudian theory was then. Two relatively competitive bodies of theory could not occupy the same space in social casework theory at the same time. It has only been relatively recently that social science knowledge has begun to provide for either a coherent view of society or useful theories of the person in society.

Along with its search for theories of the person in society, social casework also developed theories of practice. The three major theoretical streams were *diagnostic casework,*[35] *functional casework,*[36] *and problem-solving theory.*[37] It is difficult to avoid the temptation here to review the development of these three schools of thought, for an analysis of their differences in approach to the individualizing process might prove to be fruitful in our understanding of the roots of modern casework practice. However, such an examination is really not within the scope of this book, and the reader is referred in the footnotes to appropriate theoretical texts that will describe each school of thought. It was not a wrong turn, in our view, that there

---

[35] Hamilton, Gordon, *Theory and Practice of Social Casework,* Columbia University Press, New York, First Ed., 1940, Second Edition, 1951.

[36] Taft, Jessie, *A Functional Approach to Family Casework,* University of Pennsylvania Press, Philadelphia, Pa., 1944.

[37] Perlman, Helen Harris, *Social Casework: A Problem Solving Process,* University of Chicago Press, Chicago, Ill., 1957.

was ferment in the practice of social casework, but again, it was an unfortunate historical necessity that so many years of theoretical argument preoccupied social case-workers and possibly deterred them from the one quest they all held in common. This writer has always been as-sociated with the diagnostic school of thought, and holds the opinion that it is very difficult to develop a totally eclectic view of practice when the theoretical roots are so at variance with each other. However, it is not our purpose here to make comparisons or to take sides in an internecine struggle; it is our total purpose to present a model for the individualizing practice of social work. The result of this effort will be viewed through many lenses, but just as we are trying to avoid the compartmentalization of casework, group work, and community organization methods, we will not deal here with the theoretical differences of schools of thought in social casework.

In the search for theory, social casework made a "wrong turn" in its pursuit of many labels, often substituting these for real, testable concepts. Probably, it is evidence of a growing professional practice that it seeks to name things so as to order its observations and present hypotheses for study and research. The problem comes when descriptive terms become labels and then are misconstrued as diag-nostic truths. One such label has been that of *multiproblem families*.[38] This term was dramatized by the St. Paul, Min-nesota programs[39] and in the 1950s was extremely pop-ular. Looking back, it seems that the adoption of "multi-problem family," a descriptive term for a social phenomenon that had a severe impact upon social workers of every call-ing, was a response of desperation. The "acting-out" phe-nomena were perceived as special to certain groups of clients, and the idea of the "subculture of poverty" was evolving as an explanation for the phenomenon of multi-

[38] Meyer, Carol H., "Individualizing the Multi-Problem Family," *Social Casework*, May 1963.

[39] Buell, Bradley and Associates, *Community Planning for Human Services*, Columbia University Press, New York, 1952.

problem families. Neither of these concepts as utilized, differentiated sufficiently the difference between people living out a defined "cultural way of life" and the fact of poverty itself. Yet, the concept of the *subculture of poverty* offered comfort as did the concept of multiproblem family, perhaps because the problems were so overwhelming, and social workers did not have the methodological tools to cope successfully with them. The overweaning allegiance to these categories, along with the assumptions that social work practices could resolve them indicates a "wrong turn" in our framework: promises were offered that could not be kept, the terms did not provide for other systems of ideas, and the theory was made applicable to only some people and not to all.

Moving now beyond the theoretical efforts noted in the development of casework theory, we must recall our discussion in Chapter 1 of the historically determined "wrong turn" that had an effect upon social casework practice, which was the emphasis upon specialization of settings and fields. Since 1929, when the Milford Conference joined the issue and enunciated a generic method of social casework, it has been understood that this was the desired goal. And yet, forty years later, the field at large is still struggling with solutions to the problem of conceptualizing the organization of practice. As we discussed in Chapter 1, it is still not settled that it shall be according to the skills of the worker, the client group, the method affiliation, or the problem. It is not a "wrong turn" to participate in such a struggle; the wrong turn is always in the parochialism that occurs when practitioners structure a hierarchy of values and subsequently bend their efforts to justifying it through affiliations of all kinds, agencies, associations, conferences, or informal handshakes. The era will determine the hierarchy; where once family casework reflected the popular core of practice, this was supplanted by psychiatric casework, presently to be supplanted by work with groups and communities. Our criteria are not met when any affiliation holds out promise that cannot be fulfilled, or when its organizational boundaries are pulled so tightly it cannot let

in other streams of thought, and when it becomes overspe-
cialized in its practice with but one type of client.

Finally, and on another level, social casework made a
well-intentioned "wrong turn" in its support of the U. S.
legislative amendments from 1962 on which affirmed the
relationship between public assistance and casework services. Perhaps through hindsight this is easy to say, but
hindsight was exactly what was missing when the "service
amendments" were supported. A look back at the Poor Law
philosophy established in this country at its inception
should have been enough to alert social workers that casework services connected with the provision of income maintenance could only indicate that the defects were in the
recipient and not in the social system. In any event, our
criteria were surely not met when promises could not be
kept to rehabilitate the poor, and the long association of
services and public assistance may well have excluded for
too long the awareness that income ought to be guaranteed
in some other form. Perhaps it was the failure of casework
services in public assistance that ultimately helped to clear
the way for serious political discussion about insured family
income without the accompanying requirement of rehabilitative services.

Ours has not been a lovely history in social casework,
but neither has the social and economic history of this
country been without wrong turns. Perhaps it has been dis-
couraging to begin our discussion of casework practice with
its failures, but the value of having done it this way is that
we have it out of the way and can now look at some themes
that have greater validity for today's practice. Before we
arrive at the millennium we seek, we will examine some
old themes that once were more functional for their times
than they are today, but they were not wrong turns in the
same sense as those we have just explored. The ones we
are about to consider are technical. Derived from the existing practice, the old themes were inevitable and necessary
for their time but did not serve as the basic guidelines for
the policy of casework practice. The question we must confront at each step is whether or not these technical compo-

nents are still necessary or still functional in the same depth and degree as they once were.

OLD THEMES. ARE THEY STILL APPLICABLE?

The *professional relationship* as a concept has a long history in social casework.[40] Technically, it means a controlled relationship between worker and client, so that the helping process is directed only to the client's requirements, without intrusion of the worker's personality or needs. Thus, a professional relationship differs significantly from the interactions that occur between neighbors and even other professional people who carry out tasks that supposedly do not depend upon an objective relationship with the client. This concept has been extremely useful in the practice of social casework, and it has served naturally the philosophy of practice at each given era. So, for example, there have been long periods when the professional relationship was misconstrued as the seat of transference in the helping process. The period when social casework was, to a large extent, preoccupied with intra-psychic processes brought with it exalted attention to uncovering mechanisms that would expose unconscious conflict. This direction of inquiry in the practice of casework inevitably led to the client's regression and sometimes to a full blown transference neurosis. In recent years the field has corrected for this possibility, and transference reactions are commonly held to a minimum, although they naturally occur in any relationship that is emotionally laden.[41]

---

[40] Biestock, Felix Paul, *The Casework Relationship*, Loyola University Press, Chicago, Ill., 1957.

Garrett, Annette, "The Worker-Client Relationship," *Am. J. Orthopsych.*, Vol. XIX, No. 2, 1949.

Robinson, Virginia, *A Changing Psychology in Social Work*, University of North Carolina Press, Chapel Hill, N.C., 1930.

[41] Garrett, Annette, "Transference in Casework," *The Family, J. Social Casework*, April 1941 (for classical casework approach to use of transference).

The professional relationship has served other psychological functions, as well as the aim of objectifying the interaction between worker and client. In ego terms, as opposed to the libidinal coloration we have just mentioned, the professional relationship has been viewed as serving as a testing ground for the client in order that he learn how to relate through his contact with the worker, not to promote transference but rather to serve to neutralize libidinal affect and to free the client to relate more objectively in his life situation.[42] Another function of the professional relationship in ego terms has been described as a structured situation in which the client may borrow strength from the worker, or use the worker as a behavior model.[43] We can see that the general idea of the professional relationship has changed in its uses, in accordance with the particular framework in which casework has been practiced over the years.

There obviously is real value in the objectified relationship, for without it the client might suffer exploitation in his contact with a social worker. This is one of the themes in casework that illustrates the necessity to preserve a valid concept and yet put it into modern use. The issue here is that if the professional relationship is used primarily to promote social distance or objectivity as it must when the helping process is viewed as something being done by an expert to or for another, then it may stand in the way of accommodating practices to the changing urban scene. Furthermore, if the professional relationship is viewed in narrow or precious terms, it will be less possible for practitioners to permit "sharing" clients with nonprofessional personnel. Thus in Chapter 6, when we consider the changing

---

[42] Bandler, Louise, "Some Casework Aspects of Ego Growth Through Sublimation," in *Ego-Oriented Casework*, Howard J. Parad and Roger R. Miller, eds., F.S.A.A., New York, 1963, pp. 89–107.

[43] McBroom, Elizabeth, "Adult Socialization: A Basis for Public Assistance Practice" (Mimeo) University of California, School of Social Welfare, Research Projects Office, Berkeley, Calif., Oct. 1966, pp. 52–54.

uses of social casework, we will need to re-examine the uses of the professional relationship in modern dress.

A second practice concept that must be re-evaluated in current terms is that of *motivation*. Like transference, this concept has had a long history in social casework practice.[44] Again, we can trace the evolution of this requirement for treatment as coming out of psychoanalytic theory and practice. Its use rests upon a number of assumptions, that the client to be helped feels and to an extent may articulate a sense of conflict or malaise sufficient for him to want the help available despite the pain and inconvenience entailed. The sense of conflict about one's self actually reflects a high level of personality organization. In Freudian terms, this is usually a neurotic individual. Thus the expectation of motivation for help in the client will rule out those vast increasing numbers of people who do not feel conflict about themselves and those who cannot articulate their conflict even though they may sense it. Moreover, the presence of motivation as a requisite of treatment suggests that conflict or problems will need to have occurred before the social-work practitioner can intervene. In order to utilize this notion in modern practice, it might well have to be reconceptualized in order to comply with current interests in early intervention and broader parameters of help. Willingness may be a more accurate term in this connection, but whatever motivation may become in social work practice, it will be necessary for us to re-examine it later in a newer context of practice.

A third theme that has run through social casework practice has to do with the *clinical diagnosis*. We must be clear here that we are referring only to clinical diagnosis and not to the general concept of diagnosis, about which we shall have a great deal more to say later on. The clinical concept derives of course directly from medicine, and in social casework it has referred primarily to psychoanalytic

---

[44] Oxley, Genevieve B., "The Caseworker's Expectations and Client Motivation," *Social Casework,* July 1966.

Soyer, David, "The Right to Fail," *Social Work,* July 1963.

or psychiatric definitions of personality problems. Here we are again bound by a practice that may inhibit social workers from going outside of a clinical boundary. In the first place, increasing numbers of problems to which social workers attend are not describable in clinical terms, either because the problem is presently perceived through a wider lens or because the client group may, in actuality, be outside of the psychoanalytic scope of practice and may not have been classified in clinical terms. Thus, if we are to see individualizing practice as available in the world outside the clinic, we must also begin to think preclinically or extraclinically or remain confined in practice to the clinically known, the clinically diagnosable, and usually, the clinically treatable. However, so as not to retreat from the necessity to become as expert in diagnosis as possible, we might have to reconceptualize the components of the diagnosis, reorient ourselves as to what the confines of the clinic are, and expand the diagnosis to include concerns that are greater in scope than the personality diagnosis. We shall address ourselves to this in some detail in Chapter 5.

CURRENT SITUATION IN SOCIAL CASEWORK

At the end of the 1960s, the practice of social casework presents many faces. On the one hand, technical expertise continues to develop along classical lines, where diagnostic categories are expanded and codified so that treatment can be replicated and studied.[45] Kinds and levels of treatment have been developed[46] toward an increasingly common language, where it is now possible for practitioners to identify these components of practice and to communicate on a rather high theoretical level. So much work has, in fact, been invested in the development of diagnostic and treatment categories, that it may be necessary to backtrack

---

[45] Turner, Francis J., ed., *Differential Diagnosis and Treatment,* Free Press, New York, 1969.

[46] Hollis, Florence, *Casework—A Psychosocial Therapy,* Random House, New York, 1964.

and re-evaluate the uses to which this technical expertise may be put. For, as we listen to the criticisms of social casework practice, examine the results of research, and place social casework in the context of urban life, it seems as if this expertise is in a hiatus and may be in need of a new framework.

There are other currents being expressed as well in social casework. These are not conceptualized to the same degree as are diagnostic and treatment techniques, and they can be viewed more as immediate responses to the urban situation. Here, we may refer to new uses of rather traditional practices in social casework, for example, home visits, expanded use of homemakers, and "reaching out techniques." Although new uses of these techniques reflect the changing society, they too need to be placed in a framework that will give them significance, for in and of themselves they cannot constitute the intellectual core of social work practice.

A third development in modern social casework practice is the marked increase in theoretical formulations toward the goal of evolving models of practice. In Chapter 6 we will deal with these models as we probe the possibility of creating a framework that will provide for relevant social work practice in the modern urban world. To date the social casework practice model has been fashioned primarily after medical practice, with attention to treatment and cure or rehabilitation. The advance of practice techniques gives evidence of the pursuit of this model. The question confronting us here is not the suitability of the techniques but rather the suitability of the model itself.

SUMMARY

We have in this section reviewed the critical state of social work practice. We have noted the popular and professional criticisms of practice and some organizational responses to practice failures. We have cited some of the reasons for some wrong turns as deriving essentially

from historical necessity, as well as from professional parochialism. Yet there is a characteristic of all social work
methods that has saved practice and has in fact created the
demand for increasing numbers of social workers. Social
work is an open system of ideas; it has in the past reflected
new knowledge and new social conditions, and it has no
inherent commitment to viewing the world as flat. Its
greatest viability lies in its ability to accommodate to
changing perceptions.

3

the urban condition

This is a bright mundo, my streets, my barrio
de noche,
With its thousands of lights, hundreds of
millions of colors
Mingling with noises, swinging street sounds
of cars and curses,
Sounds of joys and sobs that make music.
If anyone listens real close, he can hear its
heart beat.

——Piri Thomas[47]

[47] Thomas, Piri, *Down These Mean Streets*, Signet Books, N.Y. 1968,
Prologue.

THE ENVIRONMENT

THE CITY IS THE WAY WE VIEW IT, each of us, depending upon the window out of which we look. There are tree-lined streets still in cities, where people enjoy some measure of peace. There, buses may not pass by the house, and yet public transportation is nearby. Rents are high so policemen ride around in prowl cars reassuringly. The garbage is collected regularly. Public utilities are serviced, and there may even be a pleasant park where the children can play. In this part of a city there may be a small public library, perhaps an art cinema, and just enough small shops and food stores that cater exactly to the needs of the people in the neighborhood. This description may sound like a suburb, for it has some of the same characteristics of pleasant living, except that it does not require commutation to a job and is ordinarily more heterogeneous in population composition.

There are other parts of the city where people live in increasing numbers, which bears as little resemblance to that pleasant neighborhood as to the suburb. Some cities might call it uptown, and others will call it downtown; in small towns the area is called "across the railroad tracks." Over time there never has been a conglomerate population in a city that did not divide itself in such ways, for the location of one's home is usually the chief indicator of one's economic class, and the marked differences between privileged and deprived people are never so evident as in the kinds of neighborhoods and houses in which they live through choice or necessity.

The uptown area of a city may be a ghetto that contains people of one particular culture, race or economic class, and, in the case of minority groups, the most descriptive characteristic of a ghetto is its poverty. Here are either old rundown houses, once owned privately and lived in by people who have long since fled to pleasanter places, leaving the houses in turn to those populations who follow, much like poor children wear hand-me-down clothes. No matter how good the clothes were when they were new, the long use and outdatedness make them shoddy wearing for the child who inherits them. Uptown also has tenements, once built to house large numbers of immigrant people who came to the city for jobs, for opportunities, and for freedom. Sometimes people have found these things and have then left the tenements, but they have always been replaced by new groups hoping to make the same circuit from their original prison, through the tenement prison and out into the wider world of space, quiet and beauty. In the meantime, tenement living has served its purpose of sheltering large numbers of people and families while they wait, perhaps for generations, to get out. Tenements built in the 19th century are generally not rebuilt to make them habitable for today, partly because nobody really thinks very much of them, and they are considered an urban blight that should not exist. But they do exist in this country in numbers that are astronomical for the state of our economy.[48]

There is a third kind of housing in the uptown area that is called public housing. In the last thirty years, since the government entered the field of housing through federal, state, and local subsidization, housing projects have developed throughout slum areas in all cities. Without addressing ourselves to the architectural standards of these projects, which have been called variously, "Mussolini modern," "prison yellow," and the like, we need to understand something about the social characteristics of this kind of living, because increasingly the poor people of this country who live in cities are forced through lack of other options to live in these projects.[49] Theoretically, publicly subsidized housing projects are the only way in which cities can be

---

[48] *Housing and Urban Development Statistics Yearbook 1966*, H.U.D. Washington, D.C.

G.S. Table 78, p. 76: the 1960 census of housing defined almost 8½ million substandard owner and renter occupied dwellings out of a little over 53 million occupied units.

[49] *Ibid.*, Table 2, p. 256: 4,386 low-rent public housing projects under management in Dec. 1966.

made habitable for people on all economic levels; they do not need to be designed with a pen dipped in the ink of the notion of less-eligibility. They might even be beautiful, six-storied or high-rise, in poured concrete and steel or in brick. Theoretically, urban planners and architects need not be confined to ugly models; we know that there are infinite possibilities of design and arrangement, but that lack of respect for the lower economic classes who rely on project living, and lack of imagination, public support, and funding have pressed the unfortunate mold of public housing that is typically seen in most large American cities. It is difficult to talk about the social aspects of public housing without commenting upon the physical aspects, because they are so intertwined for the person who must live in a project. A cheerless project building is an affront to its tenant, just as an unpainted and run-down frame house troubles its owner in a rural area. More so, because the tenant cannot do anything about his building and he must take what comes, no matter the sense of indignity it offers.

As to the way of life in a public housing project, this must concern us in a different way than the way of life pursued by any of us in any other economic class or neighborhood, because what we do freely on our own terms describes our individuality, but where an organization, in this case, a public housing authority, defines acceptable behavior in arbitrary terms, we must evaluate the organization in order to understand the individual's behavior. For example, when public housing projects determine the rules of entry, they are really setting standards of living that quite surpass their purposes. Neither a private landlord nor a public housing authority manager should be able to decide to keep out of his building an unmarried mother merely because he disapproves of her single status. In most states this practice will be illegal, and yet it occurs often as private and public policy. The rules devised by public housing authorities are supposedly directed to mollifying the inherent strains of group living, and yet who is to say that such living would be eased or not by allowing children's pets, permitting running in the halls, and tolerating social behavior that is syntonic to the times in which we are living? When a certain proportion of the population at large is delinquent, criminal, addictive, or antisocial in other ways, eviction from public housing is not a proper solution to these problems. Eviction can only make the social conditions that created the problem even more deplorable. If the rules of society have not succeeded in controlling some behaviors, the arbitrary rules of conduct devised by public housing authorities are not necessarily more successful, to say nothing of their injustice. To be just is to apply the same rules to all. Where one child in a private dwelling is subject only to the rules of the society at large through its legal institutions, then it is unjust when a child living in publicly supported housing is subject to restrictions on his living, as well as to legitimate social restraints. Under such restrictions do poor people live even when they live in public housing projects.

Taking all forms of residence together, where poor people live is the slum area of any city. As middle-class people reach out to suburban areas, their places are quickly taken by these people who are captives of the city and the so called inner-city areas have consequently enlarged to encompass increasingly the total geography of the city.⁵⁰ Slums are crowded, because that is their function—to house large numbers of people in as small a place as possible. Slums are dirty, partly because some people who are new immigrants to the city come from rural areas,⁵¹ and they are not accustomed to the complexities of sanitation systems, nor are they used to the accumulation of dirt and garbage that occurs in all sectors of the city. Moreover, slums are dirty because there is less regular garbage collection and

---

⁵⁰ *Ibid.,* G.S. Table 63, p. 65: In re: white and nonwhite people living inside central cities between 1950–1960 . . . there was a 10.8% increase in this period . . . 4.7% white and 51% nonwhite increase.

⁵¹ *Ibid.,* G.S. Table 76, p. 74: Of the total population in 1965, 338,000 who lived in the South were living in the Northeast, for example, in 1966.

because people in slums live in their streets and inevitably create clutter. Slums are dangerous because crowdedness and the prevalence of poverty create conditions where delinquency, crime, and drug addiction thrive. Slums are expensive because poor people must pay the exclusive costs of private enterprise in every area of their lives. Also, they are restricted to their neighborhoods because of lack of carfare, lack of baby sitters, and lack of acceptance downtown, so they must deal in stores around them and not participate in the downtown bargains.

As for the social institutions, more than in any other area of the city, people in the slums rely upon public provision of health, education, and welfare services. Except for the presence of churches and some voluntary community action projects, people who live in slum areas do not use private schools, private social agencies, or private hospitals and clinics. First, there are negligible numbers of these private organizations that exist in slum areas, and second, poor people cannot pay the fees for private services even when such facilities are located nearby. Third, it is possible that discriminatory practices would rule poor people out of use of private facilities, even where the first two conditions did not exist. Thus public facilities are the major source of vital help to the vast numbers of people living in city slum areas. We will discuss in Chapter 4 the question of public and private auspices, including some of the differences among local, state and federal agencies, but in this more or less pictorial account of city living, we shall comment only upon the way these social institutions appear. The local public school, hospital, and welfare agency are typically, except for demonstration showcase projects, the oldest and worst buildings of their kind in the city. Reflecting the conditions of slum life, they are not much better, even though they are usually administered by people who do not come from the slums themselves. In other words, these public institutions are crowded, dirty, and dangerous. Like public housing they must reflect to the poor population exactly what society at large thinks about poor people, for they do not show a good face, they do not respect the human spirit, they do not recognize the individuality of a person, and they do not seem to improve at any pace, despite all the criticism expressed by humanitarians everywhere.

Slum living in the city means more than being poor. In every civilization poverty has carried its particular burdens, so that as a condition of life it has been harrowing for the 18th-century Londoner and the 20th-century Mississippian. There never was any glory in being poor, despite the romantic and religious teachings to the contrary, and being poor has had historically a spiraling effect upon the individual. His poverty has kept him hungry and deprived of all other basic necessities of life, but more, it has chained him to the leavings of the society at large—all of the institutional hand-me-downs finally belong to the poor. Yet, slum living is more than even that; it is a living and breathing daily reminder to the individual that in an affluent society he is deprived and denigrated. In a mobile society, he is trapped within his neighborhood. In a materialistic society, he is without any of its concrete rewards. In an increasingly educated society that is tooling up for the post-cybernetic age, he is illiterate. In a society that strives for superior medical care, he is the sickest both mentally and physically. In a society that reaches the moon, he must cling to his outmoded fire escape. The slum is poverty, but more than that, it is everything that is old-fashioned in a modern society; it is a massive expression of cultural lag that is knowingly supported by the total society that lives outside of it. Moreover, the environmental ills that affect all people who live in the city affect the slum dweller more intimately, because he cannot ever find alternate modes of living or afford compensatory mechanisms to deal with them.

As we turn to the conditions of urban life that affect "everybody" we must first explore the midtown neighborhood that houses the middle-class population who still live in the cities. Here, we will include the commuters who daily use the city's facilities and who populate the downtown offices that are integral to the life of the city. Aside from the decreasing numbers of small houses in cities,

middle- and upper-class people live in all varieties of apart-
ments, and they pay rents that range beyond count from
low to high and even higher. The plight of the middle-class
city resident is well known: he must pay too large a proportion of his income for his rent, and he can seldom find
sufficient room or a satisfactory arrangement of space, light,
air, convenience, and safety. He is not restricted in area as
is the slum or ghetto dweller, but often he is wrongly
viewed as if he were as free to take the city's offerings as
the high income city dweller. He does not share the restrictions or the squalor of the poor resident, but neither does
he find the kind of accommodation in housing that makes
for a pleasurable life. He suffers along with every other
city resident from air pollution, outdated public transportation facilities, jammed traffic, an ear-piercing decibel
count in the streets, overcrowding in schools, hospitals,
clinics, social agencies, department stores, and supermar-
kets. His troubles, when compared to the troubles of the
poor, are not as fundamental in life, in that he can afford
to cope better with the inherent problems of urban life, but
in truth every city dweller shares in its strains. The modern
city is a place where people are born or are required to live
for many reasons. To the degree that people live there in
order to seek freedom and pursue their interests of whatever kind, the price one must pay for these opportunities is
costly when it is measured in terms of human health and
personal dignity. Why then, do so many people live in the
cities,[52] and what is to be their fate?

WHY PEOPLE LIVE IN CITIES

"The city has always welcomed men in search
of services."[53] As the demand for services outgrew the possibility of their provision in smaller units, cities have served

---

[52] *Ibid.*, G.S. Table 63, p. 65: In 1966, over 125 million people (out
of over 194 million population) lived in metropolitan areas; an
increase of 26.4% between 1950 and 1960.

[53] Yarmolinsky, Adam, "The Service Society," in *The Conscience of
the City, Daedalus,* Fall 1968, p. 1263.

their function as the clearinghouse for experts in everything. It has been said that "in the city every occupation, including mendicancy and prostitution, tends to become a profession."[54] It is well known that most of the technical innovations presently available came into being within the last fifty years; thus, the burgeoning of knowledge has made it imperative for specialization to occur. For example, on one city block, there may be a repairman for radios, television sets, kitchen appliances, and electrical wiring. There is no longer a general electrician, any more than there is a general doctor who could possibly know everything necessary in medicine. The presence of massive populations who have come to cities in the last fifty years have in themselves created the demand for services simply in order to be able to exist together. So, for example, cities provide a range of services from police to transportation and sanitation—services that derive from conglomerate living. Moreover, as our society has perfected its production of goods through mechanical means, services have become the major employment outlet for increasing numbers of people. In other words, people join together to make the most economic use of each other's services, and then services become the end product as their provision becomes utilitarian for people. The vast increase in range and complexity of services in this century has characterized urban living both advantageously and, where services contradict rather than complement each other, disadvantageously. In all cases, however, the availability of services affects the popularity of individual cities.

> The urban environment . . . is a medium for transmitting the form and content of contemporary society, a territory to be explored, and a setting for the testing of identity.[55]

---

[54] Martindale, Don, "Prefatory Remarks," *The City*, Max Weber, Free Press, New York, 1968, p. 53.

[55] Carr, Stephen and Lynch, Kevin, "Where Learning Happens," *The Conscience of the City, Daedalus*, Fall 1968, p. 1279.

We shall have more to say later about the changing role of the family in society, but here it should be noted that as the influence of family declines, a nation's culture and tradition are made explicit through the larger social environment. Although urban life might be considered as the root of our present social evils, it is also the source of a rich variety of experience, offering to all citizens untold more stimuli than families ever could provide. Perhaps this phenomenon helps to explain why young people so often choose to find their interests outside of their family life. The city not only provides cultural experiences through its theaters, movie houses, concert halls, and museums, it also arranges for every possible kind of entertainment, social exchange, and above all difference, so that city dwellers need merely look for and find opportunities to pursue their natural style of life. It is this individualized landscape that draws people together, making the crowded urban environment a highly personal experience. The ready accessibility of all of the familiar social, educational, and physical experiences in the city offers to people a diverse way of life, but it carries with it the looming potential of getting lost and overwhelmed. As with the service possibilities, so the stimuli of the city and the opportunities to pursue one's individual identity may create tension when one does not know exactly what one's identity is, nor where to look for it.

Cities have grown in America since the Civil War, and the urban way of life has become typical for 96 million people in this country, or 53% of the population who occupy only 0.7% of the nation's land, all concentrated in but 213 urban areas.[56] Furthermore, of the 196.6 million people in America, 70% live in urban centers and half of this number are under thirty.[57] The process of urbanization has been going on for 5000 years, but only in the last fifty years

[56] Davis, Kingsley, "The Urbanization of the Human Population," *Cities*, Dennis Flannagan, ed., Alfred A. Knopf, New York, 1965, pp. 3–24.

[57] *Pocket Data Book U.S.A.*, U.S. Government Printing Office, 1967, p. 5.

have migrations and technological change occurred at such a pace that the urban way of life has become for many a problem way of life. The great attraction of ethnic and racial diversity has turned into a nightmare of interpersonal conflict. The opportunity for individual freedom has turned into a roller coaster for turned-on youth. The availability of cultural pursuits and entertainment has turned into a massive traffic jam in the streets and at the ticket windows. The presence of educational advantages has turned into a political struggle for the minds of the young. The hope for almost unlimited employment opportunities built upon service systems has turned into an organizational pot-pourri, so that people cannot get work even though their labor is necessary for the city to thrive. Equally important, the services themselves do not reach the citizen at large. It seems that our laissez-faire attitudes have countermanded the obvious necessity for planning in all areas of urban living, and the result is the near chaos that is presently being called the urban crisis. In order to draw implications for social work practice in this urban crisis, we must look more closely at some of the problems before us.

PROBLEMS OF POWER RELATIONSHIPS

The increasing numbers of black, Puerto Rican, Mexican, American Indian and other people who have moved to urban communities have enhanced the inevitable strife that occurs when the haves and have-nots confront each other. Cities have always been the first resting place, at least in coastal areas, for foreign immigrants, and there has always been the strain accompanying the confrontation of new peoples with the older citizens. The strain comes from economic dependency and differences in living habits and cultures alien to the existing one. However, in the early part of this century there were differences that mitigated the power conflicts that are now occurring in the last half of the century. In the first place the European and the Asian immigrant brought with them the cultures they had had in their own countries. Thus they belonged to each other and had allegiances with the past that helped them to thrive in a new country and to find an identity. Secondly, the major foreign immigrations occurred before World War I and before the end of the industrial and the beginning of the technical era. In 1890 a mere one-fifth of the urban population was foreign born. There were job opportunities in factories, for example, that were commensurate with potential skills of the immigrant people, and they organized through unions and other associations to protect their labor. Third, except for Oriental people who have been a minority in this country, most of the immigrants from abroad were Caucasian. Thus, except for habits of living and language, which could be changed in only one generation, they could find their way into the major society through integration. Despite the burdens they carried and the discrimination they met, sooner or later they could become part of all that was going on in their new world.

The situation is presently quite different inasmuch as the ethnic minorities who have replaced the Europeans in cities are for the most part of all different colors, which makes their integration into the mainstream of society difficult when that society is one that protects the apparent purity of its race. In the first place, nonwhite people are excluded through a range of discriminatory measures *because* of their color, and in the second place, the factor of color makes nonwhite people visible, and thus they cannot avoid the separatism forced upon them by the white community at large. It is now more than a case of haves vs. have-nots, because the deprivation suffered by nonwhites is so pervasive, that there is not even sufficient opportunity or hope toward which they can strive. As the U.S. Report on Civil Disorders states:

> Negroes could point to the doctrine of white supremacy, its widespread acceptance, its persistence after emancipation and its influence on the definition of the place of Negroes in American life. They could point to their long fight for full citizenship, when they had active opposition

from most of the white population and little or no support from the government.[58]

The lack of federal planning and responsibility for programs that would equalize the income and employment opportunities throughout the country have made it imperative for poor blacks, Puerto Ricans, Mexican-Americans, and American Indians to migrate from mainly rural areas north to the urban centers in the country. They have come in large numbers and have gained a little economic security in exchange for tremendous social losses.

> I want to talk about the experiences of a misplaced generation, of a misplaced people in an extremely complex, confused society. This is a story of their searching, their dreams, their sorrows, their small and futile rebellions, and their endless battle to establish their own place in America's greatest metropolis . . . and in America itself.[59]

So eloquently did Claude Brown describe the plight of the southern black who came to New York City. And what did they bring, and what did they find?

Black migrants have come from southern rural areas where their reliance on the land that no longer provided a living kept them connected with the slave milieu that is a mere 100 years past. Due to the formula of public assistance payments where individual states determine their own budgets, wealthy states like New York for example, could hold out a better living grant than could poor states like Mississippi, and this difference contributed to the migration north. Also, in the early half of this century, going north was thought to be a step forward to employment opportunities that provided for more mobility than farming. It has been "where the action is" and has drawn young poeple to it to find that action. So they came, as did the Puerto Ricans

---

[58] *Report of the National Advisory Commission on Civil Disorders,* Bantam Books, New York, March 1968, p. 235.
[59] Brown, Claude V., *Manchild in the Promised Land,* Signet Books, New York, 1966, p. vii.

from rural areas and poor cities, and the Indians from despicable reservations, and Mexican-Americans from useless productivity.

They brought with them their lives and their families, but little else. How could they have been prepared for the crowds, the dirt, the temptations of drugs, the complicated requirements of sanitation facilities, indoor plumbing and the terrible distances between work and home? How could they have known about the rules imposed upon all city people, the reliance upon organizations, the socially distant professional behavior of people in schools, hospitals, and social agencies, and the cruelty of strangeness? How could they have been prepared for unemployment, underemployment, continuing poverty in spite of the promise of some new kind of comfort in the city?

After the Civil Rights Bill was passed in the Congress in 1964, it became evident that black people were not going to gain with any speed the rights of access to good schools, housing, employment, medical care or social services; integration of black and white people in a society of equal opportunities was viewed by many as a dream. The major crisis of cities evolved at the point that black leadership began to assert Black Power, which probably was the only possible course of action for a long-time oppressed people who could wait no longer for their civil rights. While Black Power has been interpreted to mean a range of things from extreme nationalism and separatism to community control of schools, it is seen increasingly as a force that is necessary for black people to find identity as individuals in an alien white society. Whereas European migrants carried with them this vital sense of identity and created their own power subsystems in this country, it cannot be forgotten that black people were physically prevented from achieving such a sense of community, by 250 years of slavery and an ensuing 100 years of being second-class citizens. Thus, if they were to become a political group with legitimate demands upon the society, a creation like Black Power was needed to take the place of the sense of community that came naturally to the European white immigrants. It is the presence now of Black Power and the demand of almost 11% of the people in this country that they control their own lives and organizations that has changed the course of the urban condition in the last very few years. Black Power frequently means that white people are viewed as suspect and, in many instances, not capable of being of service to black people; Black Power means literal control of social institutions that have been proved to be nonserving and dysfunctional for black people. This is, indeed, a social crisis, for black people are becoming the majority group in northern cities, and the institutions that serve them and all other people are generally staffed by white people even while menial tasks continue to be carried out by blacks. The crisis has a deeper dimension, for it also expresses a revolt of citizens against organizations, possibly because they have been so long identified with disregard for black individualism. Thus, one hears the demand for community control, decentralization, neighborhood storefronts, outreach centers, and for all forms of social utilities that do not reflect the larger systems. This is surely an organizational crisis, because most social, educational and health services have developed historically into larger and larger organizational systems. The crisis in cities is but a few steps short of an active revolution to which there must be a reasonable response.

YOUTH AND THEIR REVOLT

It is not possible to generalize about youth as a group, because they are not organized into militant power groups as are the blacks. It is understood that every generation has had its gap between parents and children, but in this era the gap is supported by waning influences of family life, diminishing regard for authority, increasing freedom from traditional mores and behavioral restraints, increasing access to drugs, greater mobility within the city, and a remarkable development in sophistication of young people, perhaps as a result of greater mobility, urban living, and exposure to television and paperback books. These events have created an unofficial power group that we call Youth. The hallmark of this generation is that youth is no longer identified as part of family life; we must learn to count individuals when we concern ourselves with young people, for the city has made it possible for them to be self-reliant and identifiable quite apart from their families. Why does the emergence of Youth as a power group contribute to the urban crisis? Because they, like Black Power groups, will no longer accept the offers of adult society to provide services, care, or education; participation in what is happening to them is the demand they make, and this demand will have its effect upon the current state of organizational life. Young people have their subcultures and, as any middle-aged social worker, teacher, or psychiatrist knows, their own language and criteria for trust and identification. This has always been so, but never to the extent now apparent, because all media in the community depict the demands of young people. When popular articles decry the "alienation of youth" perhaps they mean the increasing alienation of the middle-aged.

What has the development of urban youth power to do with a crisis in service institutions? The Boy Scouts, the YMCA, community centers, and settlements may, indeed, belong to a quieter age, a rural, homogeneous, post-Victorian era. What have they now to do with student revolts on the campus, with Hippies, with high-school students who refuse to go to school and who take LSD? Institutions take a long time to change, but the revolution in style is already here, and the impasse between the warring groups of institutions and Youth is indeed a social crisis of the largest order.

It has been noted that a small percentage of the population will increasingly have the ability or inclination to upset or perturb the system: "the population of urban environments will be so large that even small percentages will represent politically and socially significant numbers of people."[60]

---

[60] Micheal, Donald N., "On Coping with Complexity: Planning and Politics," *The Conscience of the City, Daedalus,* Fall 1968, p. 1180.

Melvin Tumin has said,

> At every level of social interaction a revolutionary struggle is taking place to eliminate the conditions that generate compliance and conformity and to foster those that make genuine consent possible.[61]

He makes the further and most interesting observation that traditional power relationships are no longer functional in a day when "former underdogs have become top dogs." The traditional direction of power has been reversed between women and men, children and parents, blacks and whites, poor and rich, criminals and police, and clients and professionals. This is a heavy thought and bears close relevance to the subject we are addressing in this book. The question before us is whether or not traditional professional social work methods, or any professional practices can be functional in the modern world, when those methods and practices have derived from an era when power relationships were of a different kind. The role of expertise has changed radically, and prior acceptance of most professional practices has relied on a quite different kind of adherence to the authority of knowledge. The "establishment" is organized to function differently than the present new culture with its relaxed restraints, its rebellion against a computerized, mechanized society, and its search for individual expression.

FACING THE FACT OF MONEY

One of the most important results of the transition from a rural to an urban way of life is the increased reliance of individuals upon money income. Living in the city means that one cannot grow one's own food, wear simple clothes, or go without shoes; nor can a family build its own house on a corner of land and take care of its maintenance. Moreover, due to the increasing complexity

---

[61] Tumin, Melvin, "Captives, Consensus, and Conflict," in *Social Theory and Social Invention,* Herman D. Stein, ed., Case Western Reserve Press, Cleveland, Ohio, 1968, p. 102.

of technology and the requisite division of labor, it has become necessary for all people to rely upon a wide range of services that cost money. Living in the city requires a mode of dress, social behavior, and expenses that were hitherto not necessary to life on the farm or even in the small town. "Within the city life has been transformed from a struggle for a livelihood with nature into an interhuman struggle for gain."[62]

There are only limited ways in which people may get money, which is the rock-bottom necessity for living in the city. They may earn it entirely through work, or through subsidization of their work, they may enter the social insurance scheme of the nation and be insured for the natural risks of industrial life, and/or they may subscribe to the residual public assistance programs for income supplementation. Whatever the mode of income maintenance, people must have that income. There are a series of issues having to do with the values placed upon work in this country. Sooner or later America will have to contemplate questions having to do with guaranteed employment and with government serving as the employer of first or last resort. We will need to cope creatively with automation, the shorter work week, and our inability to know how to use leisure time. We will need to accept the fact that everyone cannot work, particularly the very old, some mothers of young children, the severely emotionally or physically disabled, and the technologically unemployable man. Is the day very far off when puritan values held in America about work will have to give way to acceptance that the necessity for money income in an urban society may be overriding and that income may have to derive from sources other than work? Whatever the choices among various guaranteed income schemes like family allowances, negative income tax, or demogrants, since income is vital to urban living, there must be public provision for families to have income so that they can survive. As we mentioned in the introduction,

---

[62] Martindale, *Op. cit.*, p. 34.

the eradication of poverty must be the first priority in this country, or we cannot talk about social work practice at all. We must emphasize the requirement of money in our discussion of urban living, because we know that it is impossible to exist in the city without it, not only because food, clothing, and shelter cannot be attained through any other means known, but also because the urban scene is typically defined by distances that have to be traveled through transportation that costs money; there is a negligible amount of recreation that is free; in short, in order to benefit from the very services the city is expected to supply, life revolves around financial transactions.

Before we consider some solutions to the urban crisis that we have touched upon, let us take a panoramic look at the city of the imminent 1970s, so that we know exactly what it is that is creating the crisis for all people. There are economic class differences, of course, that are fundamental to the crisis before us. A decreasing number of individuals who live in cities can afford all or most of the comforts of life, and yet they too suffer from the outrageous environment, i.e., air pollution, crowds, faulty transportation systems, unpleasant architecture, and loss of connections with each other and with the society around them. Moreover, they too feel the impact of social upheaval, transfer of power, and faltering institutions; they too react with fears of revolt, crime, and drug use. The poor black, Puerto Rican, Mexican, and Indian people feel all of these strains and more, because they do not have the money to cope with its effects and are too often hungry. In our culture, work has the highest priority not only as the means to earn an income and for nation-building but also because of its long-felt ethical value as character-building. Yet, unemployment figures may rise as high as 6% at the same time that the unemployed are considered to be second-class citizens. When people do go to work, there are insufficient facilities for the care of their children. When people get sick, they must wait a very long time at clinics, and they do not universally receive the best available treatment. When they go to school, they do not get the best professional education, and parents have come to feel that children are not being educated for the real world in specific cultural terms. Unions, politicians, professionals, civil servants, all representing the range of establishments, seem to be at war with the people they are there to serve. The machine seems to have broken down; is there any way to fix it?

REDEFINITIONS . . . PSYCHO-SOCIAL TO ECOLOGICAL THINKING

There is a long tradition in sociology, urban planning, economics, and architecture to define the urban environment in geographical or spatial terms, when, in fact, the city is more than a series of types of environment. Cities are defined geographically as inner cities, megalopolises, linkages of cities, and slums and so forth, and yet these terms do not help us to understand them. It is equally absurd to describe cities as a collection of neighborhoods, when urban redevelopment and other causes of mobility contradict the neighborhood concept. The modern city is more than a market place and less than a community; it is less than a collection of social systems and more than a conglomerate of individuals and small groups; it is more than a local, politically autonomous environment, and it is less than an expression of a grand national scheme. It seems hopeless to assign spatial definitions, and no comprehensive definition would meet the requirements of all of the urban specialists and particular interest groups. "In a large city there are a multitude of overlapping jurisdictions and every functional component of a city has its own zone of influence . . . ."[63] This explanation would clarify the functions and structures of theaters, jobs, neighborhoods, and social institutions that may be far across town and yet serve a particular individual or group of individuals. In any event, it has been noted that "The American city has always

---

[63] Tunnard, Christopher, *The Modern American City*, Van Nostrand Co. Inc., Princeton, N.J., 1968, p. 10.

been a place where things ought to be better than they are." There is observable evidence that there is no geographical conception of the city possible, except perhaps for the slums which are "place-defined communities." Thus it would be more cogent to define cities in terms of "life space" and address social service programs accordingly.

People tend to cluster about their functional interests, sometimes around buildings that house specialized industries, political and legal centers, barrios where tropical foods are sold, or black ghettos where people feel equal to each other. The interest in maintaining geographical organization as the pivotal concept in cities has been described by Yarmolinsky as an expression of "the inconvenience of the serving agency over the person being served . . . . Clinics are in hospitals; parks and playgrounds are in other people's neighborhoods."[64] As organizations tend to be grouped away from the people whom they should serve, it has become necessary in recent years to erect "out-reach" and "satellite" structures in order to countermand that tendency.

In viewing the boundaries within a city that tend to define the life style of the inhabitants, it is important to reiterate that lower-class people are always more reliant than other income groups upon public and sometimes voluntary service organizations. One must therefore be more alert to the locations of these services. Lyle Fitch has said:

> Middle and higher income people are highly mobile; their roots tend to be in professional, cultural, and other interests rather than in the geographical neighborhoods where they happen to be living at the moment . . . the middle class can, and frequently does, escape by moving to the suburbs where its members spend much of their civic energy building fortifications against incursions by the poor.[65]

In a sense, the poor in the city are land-locked; they are forced to live on terms that are defined for them by politics,

---

[64] Yarmolinsky, *Op. cit.,* p. 1267.

[65] Fitch, Lyle C., "Eight Goals for an Urbanizing America," *The Conscience of the City, Daedalus,* Fall 1968, p. 1146.

public welfare, hospitals, schools, business, and all other social and economic institutions that they do not necessarily structure by and for themselves. It would seem evident that social work practitioners need to be located exactly in those varied institutions where people go. Whereas the middle class may define their "neighborhoods" in accordance with its economic ability and special interests, the poor man's "neighborhood" seems to be defined by the presence of services.

PARTICIPATION AS A REALITY

> Development is whatever increases the individual's involvement in self-motivated choice and action, whatever increases his power to formulate and execute personal intentions, whether delighting in the moment or planning a course of life.[66]

Assuming that the development of the individual is a fundamental social aim in our present world, this statement provides the rationale and possibly the major guideline for participation of people in the programs of their lives. The complexity of human life in the city tends to freeze people in defensive molds, probably so that they can better cope with the continuing contextual contrasts around them. It would seem that society's present efforts to raise the influence of the individual partially reflect the growing feeling of threat of the emerging Orwellian man of 1984. If technological change is to make it decreasingly possible or necessary for man to control his environment and the things around him, then society will need to compensate through opening avenues for man, at the very least, to control his personal and social destiny. Where are the opportunities that might be made available to him? Except for his ballot and participation in occasional mass protests it is unlikely that the individual can affect the large national decisions that control his life, such as the nation's involvement in wars, in space races, in tax policies, in government

---

[66] Carr, Lynch, *Op. cit.*, p. 1278.

welfare programs, etc. Also it would be hopeless to strive for individual man's control over electrical power failures, television programing, or the proportions of steel to concrete in a skyscraper. But what can man control in relevant ways? What, in fact, is his business in particular? What affects him personally and is therefore in the arena of his competence? What aspects of his life must he participate in to maintain his integrity as a person with individuality?

The traditional American expressions of man's legal right to his own decisions have been in such intimate matters as his choices of friends, lovers, and marriage partners, his decisions about the number of children he wants to have, and how he will conduct his life inside his home. His affectional decisions might not always be under his conscious control, but they will be his by nature, and he will be able to express them as long as they do not conflict with the law. For example, he may beat his wife as long as she does not go to court to sue him for cruelty, or he may neglect his children, as long as the terms of his neglect are not defined in the statutes. Furthermore, during the minority of his children, a parent may make certain decisions about their conduct, their discipline, their schooling, their social lives, their decision to marry and so forth, to the degree that his relationship with his children makes it possible. Thus, internal, family, and affectional choices are typically expected to belong entirely to the individual, within certain broadly prescribed legal and behavioral requirements. This is understood in a democratic society, that the public through government, police, listening device, or any investigative arm is not permitted constitutionally to invade the privacy of an individual's home, although we often note breaches in enforcement of these rights. To a large extent most individuals in our society do enjoy or at the least expect these rights of personal freedom, and they are not ordinarily contested.

But what of the individual's rights to participation in his own destiny when he steps out of the confines of his home and his relationships expand to include the outer society and its social institutions? In the courts, his rights are prescribed by law and judicial interpretation that are subject to higher court review. There is innate protection built into the law for the individual to participate in his own behalf, even though there are instances when the legal process breaks down. Nevertheless, the intent of the legal system in this country is to provide participatory opportunities for every individual equally. Social Security as an institution of society also defines clearly the ground rules for a person's participation in the program; as long as he is eligible through status for a particular form of social security, he may receive it with equity. To the extent that social institutions are governed by legal statutes or universal policies that are objectively determined by the Congress or by the computer, the individual's rights as a citizen are theoretically almost as safe as they are in his home.

Difficulties seem to arise when professional expertise is in question, when decisions are made arbitrarily by specialists. Let us presume that experts in social work, medicine, teaching, housing administration, police work, school, and university administration do indeed know more about their specialties than the individual consumer of their services. When politicians, who may or may not know more about some issues, take stands, they are subject to re-election, and thus must listen to a certain extent to their constituents. In politics as in the law, the individual benefits by some measures of political control against many of the inhibitions of his life. It is not always so when it comes to professional expertise. We know that when we go to an automobile mechanic or we bring in a plumber or electrician, he is the expert and we must abide by his decision to act upon his perception of what the trouble is. If something goes wrong, we have certain limited options of our own: we cannot use him again; we can hold up his payment; or we can complain to his organization or to the Better Business Bureau or to a local authority. Nevertheless we are in a real sense at his mercy, as long as we do not have his technical competence. This kind of technical competence really belongs under the heading of things over which none of us can have direct control, because technology has surpassed our capacity to cope with all of its ramifications. We can only control the decision to use a particular technician, and then we may try to make him accountable to us.

When it comes to professional competence, the individual is faced with the same lack of knowledge of the art, science, or craft of the professional person involved. As he will increasingly require those services in this complex world, he has no choice but to seek them. It is in the area of professional competence in the personal areas of an individual's life that there are unlimited opportunities for his participation that are typically overlooked at each encounter. To a large extent this occurs because of professionalism and status requirements that seem to be requisite among experts. Often the oversight may be unintentional and may be due to overwork or organizational restraints or because participation of the client-consumer may cause trouble, take time, or be threatening to the feeling of competence held by the professional. Then again, the oversight may be due to deliberate attitudes that the individual being served is uninformed simply because he is a layman—consumer, client, or patient.

> Life is increasingly composed of impersonal components that displace personal colorations leading the individual to summon the utmost in uniqueness and particularization to preserve the personal core of the self.[67]

Where is it more appropriate for the individual to achieve this uniqueness than in the areas of his life where his very individuality is at stake?

A surgical patient needs to know what is going to happen to him and why; a parent of a school child needs to have a say in the kind of education his child is getting; a university student needs to exercise some control in the aims and conditions of his education; a community of ten-

---

[67] Martindale, *Op. cit.*, p. 34.

ants ought to arrive at a mutual decision about the rules under which they can best live together; and a client of a social worker must have free access to the rationale underlying actions taken in his behalf. We are not saying that expertise is unimportant: the teacher can teach better than the parent; the doctor has more knowledge than the patient; and the social worker understands more than his client about the meanings of the psycho-social situation in which the client exists. But as the client, patient, or student is the object of the service, he must have his chance to object, to choose, to withdraw, and to modify the actions that are happening to him. Policies and rules ought to enable the process or the service to work; policies and rules themselves are not services, and consumers should have the most to say about these.

INDIVIDUALIZATION AS A SOCIAL INVENTION

If the future could bring a resolution to the present urban crisis, we might imagine that cities would be well-designed with adequate housing and planned green areas, that rapid transportation would be clean and efficient and that private cars would not be necessary in the cities, that political institutions would be responsive to the people's real needs, that all social institutions would function expeditiously, that social utilities would be available for all people, that social insurances, health care, and education would reach the theoretical horizons already established, and that individuals would have sufficient money to live comfortable lives in a more equitable society. Admittedly, this is a future that is beyond our present dreams; in fact the urban crisis exists because of failures of our requirements in all of the areas just mentioned. Nevertheless, if we can permit ourselves to dream, and if we can truly imagine such a millennium, there would remain an inherent restraint in urban life that would not be cared for no matter how progressive our social and economic schemes. The fact of urban life that characterizes it and no other living condition is the inevitable claim of the crowded, organized, institutionalized city against the freedom and fulfillment of the individual. It is the necessity to draw this urban society to human scale that remains and will remain because of, if not in spite of, the social advances we might be able to make.

The increasing institutionalization of life has been written about by novelists and social scientists and is of course observable to everyone who has had to cope with the network of services in the city. One hears comments like, "The source of most information in the city is the telephone yellow pages." Cities by their very nature require "legal control, based on rules which are deliberate, explicit and have a special machinery for enforcement which become more prominent; the mores and the folkways less."[68] The individual must be reduced in his personal influence over his life, and yet, ironically, due precisely to this fact, he must strive himself, alone, to remain an individual doing the work of his own life, and giving expression to his own feelings. Thus the urban environment must cope with a mass society, and the individual is left to fend for himself against great odds, just exactly when he needs his individuality the most.

Ultimately, we confront the problem of selecting out of the total social system those particular provisions that will meet the needs of a particular individual. "The more complex the resulting system, the greater the need for specialized human intervention to guide people through it."[69] This has been said another way, that people "need a guide through a civilized jungle, and planning and coordination of specialized services."[70] The urban condition requires vast specialization, and at present there is no specialist in the liaison function that will connect individuals with services;

[68] Wilensky, Harold L. and Lebeaux, Charles N., *Industrial Society and Social Welfare*, Russell Sage Foundation, New York, 1958, p. 119.

[69] Yarmolinsky, *Op. cit.*, p. 1272.

[70] Wilensky and Lebeaux, *Op. cit.*, p. 14.

there is no accepted individualizer of the urban environment. It is this function that we are suggesting is the natural function of the social work practitioner.

In the next chapter we shall look more closely at the rising influence of public social institutions, and the waning impact of family life, religion, and voluntary associations. The urban society in America seems to be replacing pre-industrial, puritan, Victorian, rural modes of life. So we observe values changing, sexual roles being rearranged, inhibitions diminishing, planning turning to attention to the moment, authority being challenged, the New Left replacing the Old Left, the rise of unofficial power groups and cynicism about the industrial-military establishment. In this latter third of the 20th century, people in cities in particular are demonstrating for here and now programs, and the social niceties that belonged to even one generation ago are no longer valued. The family, the church, the school, the university, the social agency, the hospital—none of these once revered institutions are any longer autonomous in their particular functions; their authority is being challenged and yet increasingly do people rely upon their services.

Social work is but one of the social institutions that is being challenged, especially so because it among all of the others has represented a prior way of life. Its affiliation with charity pales in this day of public responsibility to guarantee a decent standard of living; its attention to intra-psychic conflict seems odd in this day of deviant acting-out, student demonstrations, and riots in the cities; its private organizations seem out of place in the increasing public control of institutions. Yet its basic values regarding the dignity of individuals, its particular expert history in helping the individual and society to get along together better, and its social aims would seem to make social work particularly qualified to carry out the task of individualization in the urban society.

4

the rise
and fall of
social institutions

*Insofar as the family as an institution turns
women into darling little slaves and men into
their chief providers and unweaned
dependents, the problem of a satisfactory
marriage remains incapable of purely private
solution. Insofar as the overdeveloped
megalopolis and the overdeveloped automobile
are built-in features of the overdeveloped
society, the issues of urban living will not be
solved by personal ingenuity and private
wealth.*

——C. Wright Mills[71]

[71] Mills, C. Wright, *The Sociological Imagination*, Grove Press, New York, 1961, p. 10.

A MAJOR PARADOX of modern urban life seems to be that while traditional social institutions like the family and the church and formal organizations like government, schools, hospitals, and social agencies are losing their public support and functional effectiveness, at the same time, people are required to rely more heavily upon these extra family services that must be available in the community. Institutionalized human services, although increasingly necessary for survival in the urban world have become almost like a bitter pill that consumers must swallow. Although it is probably not necessary to belabor the point which has become common knowledge, it might help our discussion of the extent to which change has forced upon us the requirement of services, to present some statistical evidence of the change in family structure and function. We will take pains not to identify these changes as family breakdown, because the prevalence of change would suggest not a social aberration but a different life style. One cannot characterize a social phenomenon that is so widespread as pathological; it is probably more accurate to characterize it as a shift in the structure and function of social institutions.

CHANGES IN THE ROLE OF THE FAMILY

The rate of marriages in this country increases, but so does the rate of divorce.[72] The birth rate continues to decline, but the rate of illegitimate births increases.[73] Both factors suggest that one-parent families are going to have to rely increasingly upon extra-familial social supports. There is a steady increase in the number of mothers

---

[72] *Statistical Abstract of the U.S.* U.S. Dept. of Commerce, Bureau of the Census, p. 61, Table 76: In 1920, the divorce rate was 8.0 per 1000 females, and in 1968 it was 10.6. However, the rate has never been as high as it was in 1945 at 14.4.

[73] *Ibid.,* p. 47, Table 53: In 1910 the birth rate was 30.1 per 1000 population and in 1967 the rate was 17.8, the lowest it has ever been. On the other hand, in 1940 the illegitimacy rate was 89.5 and in 1966 it was 302.4. Even accounting for the improved reporting, this is a steady increase.

of children under eighteen who work and must find outside child-caring arrangements.[74] Education begins at increasingly earlier ages and ends at later ages,[75] indicating not only that the period of adolescent dependency is prolonged, but also that children and youth increasingly are subject to extra-familial influences for more of their lives. The life-expectancy for Americans has increased markedly,[76] suggesting that health and welfare services for the aged will become highly significant as long as the aged do not continue living with their adult families.

The fact that the population in America is increasing in numbers if not proportionately and that people are living longer even though the birth rate might be declining, suggests that the crowded urban world is going to demand *quantity* health and social services. Furthermore considering that nuclear families separate more quickly from their extended families and that the time of child-rearing within the family itself has increasingly lessened, educative and socialization functions are increasingly assumed by extra-familial and public institutions. Almost as soon as the child is able to function without his mother, he comes to rely on extra-familial resources; family structures like cellular structures, proliferate into separate units very quickly in urban America. Babies are increasingly born in hospitals after their mothers have had clinical prenatal care. Infants are cared for by child-rearers who may not be their own

---

[74] *Ibid.*, p. 38, Table 44: In 1967, of all families (48,921) 58.4% had children under 18.

Social Development, U.S. Dept. of HEW, 1966, p. 89, Table 36: 32% of the mothers who work have children under 18.

[75] *Ibid.*, p. 51, Chart 47: In 1940 18% of the five year olds were enrolled in kindergarten, while in 1963, 54% were enrolled. This figure does not include those children who attend day care and Operation Headstart facilities.

Statistical Abstract, Op. cit., p. 108, Table 150: Between 1950–1966 there was a 15.8% increase of all children and youth enrolled in school at all levels.

[76] *Ibid.*, p. 53, Table 65: In 1920 the age of life expectancy was 54.1 years, and in 1966 it was 70.1 years.

mothers, in group day-care or family day-care facilities, or by baby sitters and other makeshift arrangements. Toddlers attend Headstart, nursery school, or pre-kindergarten classes, and children increasingly do not leave school until they are beyond the age of late adolescence. When children and youth are not in school, they attend organized recreational programs and, particularly in the urban environment, create their own leisure-time activities in the streets. Young adults marry earlier and have babies earlier than they used to; thus, they leave their primary families to begin the fast moving cycle again. Less and less do we find members of families depending upon each other for physical sustenance, social control, or the transmission of culture. These prior functions are carried out by extra-familial institutions.

When we look at statistical indices of psycho-social pathology in our modern society, it becomes even more apparent that individuals have come to require social institutions. Obviously, the family cannot now, nor rarely could previously, provide the specialized care that is required when one of its members is sick or disturbed or in trouble with the law. It is commonplace to accept the fact of public or institutional care for people who suffer from psycho-social pathological conditions. As population increases and urban tensions do not recede, the statistics of individual breakdown seem harrowing.

Addictions,[77] crime,[78] delinquency,[79] dependency and neglect,[80] school dropouts,[81] physical illnesses, mental ill-

[77] *Ibid.*, p. 81, Table 113 cites the annual average of *new* addicts between 1953 and 1966 as 7,615.

[78] *Ibid.*, p. 143, Table 206, citing arrest rates: There was a 62.1% increase in the number of all offenses between 1960 and 1966.

[79] *Ibid.*, p. 154, Table 228: In 1960, 20.1% per 1000 population of 10–17 year olds were adjudged delinquent. In 1966 the number was 24.8% (excluding traffic).

[80] *Ibid.*, p. 154, Table 228: The rate per 1000 population under 18 in 1966 was 2.3%. It is still not known what the rate of child abuse is.

[81] *Ibid.*, p. 114, Table 162: In 1966, the census counted 2,878 dropouts in thousands.

nesses, and the retarded,[82] are the major pathologies that have to be addressed in the urban society. Thus, we find that courts, prisons, hospitals, clinics, and family and child welfare agencies have become the modern caretakers for those people who are in trouble. Physicians, psychiatrists, social workers, nurses, therapists, and remedialists of all kinds have become the technicians of urban society whose services are absolutely necessary in light of the statistics of psycho-social pathology that command attention. The family as an institution does not have the necessary skills or resources to cope with breakdown of their individual members; help has become a public responsibility.

Returning to the population at large that does not experience the psycho-social problems we have just mentioned, it is important to recall the extent to which *all* people rely upon extra-familial organizations and institutions for their survival in the urban world. Presently, these human services are conceptualized either as residual or institutional services,[83] or as social utilities or developmental services.[84] Out of our interest in finding the place for individualizing services in the urban society, we have constructed a scheme that will describe the emerging developmental services in transaction with age groups. There is a systematic relationship between the individual and the social institutions with which he intersects at any stage of his life. We can observe this intersection through a developmental lens in accord-

---

[82] *Ibid.*, p. 74. In 1966, there were 1,248,000 patients: 527,000 hospitalized for mental disorders, 524,000 in out-patient psychiatric clinics, and 197,000 in institutions for the mentally retarded.

[83] Wilensky and Lebeaux, *Op. cit.*, p. 138. [The RESIDUAL CONCEPT] holds that social welfare institutions should come into play only when the normal structures of supply, the family, and the market, break down.

[The INSTITUTIONAL CONCEPT] in contrast, sees the welfare services as normal, "first line" functions of modern industrial society.

[84] Kahn, Alfred J., *Theory and Practice of Social Planning,* Russell Sage Foundation, New York, 1969, p. 189. "Those social utilities designed to meet the normal needs of people arising from their situations and roles in modern social life might be thought of as "developmental provision.""

ance with the natural development of the individual, or, we can view it through a residual lens when the individual presents maladaptive modes of functioning. It is possible, through such a systemic view of individuals in transaction with their environment, to note the areas in which normal anticipatory crises of age, transition, and development will occur, as well as to note where pathological crises might erupt.

We have claimed that urban living in itself is a major crisis event in which all citizens, but especially the poor and minority groups with less resources, suffer the anomic and isolated deprivation of collective living in an unplanned and unresponsive urban environment. As long as society itself is organizationally unresponsive, pathological responses on the part of individuals may actually be accommodating to the present life style of the city. Unless universal and developmental services are available at all points of intersection, it might be a nightmarish inevitability that residual and problem-focused human services would become institutional necessities for all citizens.

WHERE INDIVIDUALS AND INSTITUTIONS INTERSECT

A transactional picture of the individual facing age-specific tasks that require need-meeting social institutions must follow from the *prior assumption* that certain universal and primary physical, mental, economic, and social needs must be met for people of every age and condition of life. Thus we would begin with the requirements for food, clothing, shelter, health care, sufficient money, education, employment opportunities, provision for social insurance, and leisure-time pursuits. These are recognized to be so fundamental in a humane society, that it might seem unnecessary to even make a comment upon them. Of course the requirement of all individuals for love and intimacy and human relationships is probably the most fundamental need of all, but even such instinctive requirements tend to rely for their appropriate expression upon a bedrock of the other needs we have mentioned that have to be met. Assuming the obvious necessity for social provision in some form or another for these basic requisites of life, we can view pictorially the transactions that could and often do occur among individuals and health, education, and welfare services. The intention here is to illustrate the typical and normal transactions that occur for all people in an urban society, and it will then become clearer what the role of social work practice might be if it were to pursue a goal of *locating services where people are at the time that the services are needed.*

NORMAL INDIVIDUAL TRANSACTIONS

INDIVIDUAL DEVELOPMENTAL AGE-SPECIFIC TASKS AND NEEDS[85]*	EXPECTABLE CRISES NATURAL, TRANSITIONAL AND PATHOLOGICAL	AVAILABLE INSTITUTIONS PROVIDING SERVICES†
I. *Birth, toddler 0-3*	Role transition for parents, working mothers, absent fathers	*Prenatal care centers for medical care, advice and parent education*
Tasks: Basic trust vs. mistrust, autonomy vs. shame and doubt.	*Typical Problems:* immature parents unwanted children neglect and abuse marital conflict	*Hospitals, Clinics Well-Baby Stations Family Services Child Welfare Services*
Needs: Mothering, care, learning, verbal, & conceptual skills.		Homemakers, Home helps Day care Protection Placement

* It is evident that each stage is cumulative. People do not develop in discrete stages; there is overlapping and always residue from previous stages. Thus "and see above" (in the 3rd column) indicates that available services are applicable at all stages, whereas some are more prominent at certain times.

† It should be noted that the institution that appears most often is the school.

[85] Erikson, Erik H., *Identity and the Life Cycle, Psychological Issues,* Vol. 1, No. 1, 1959, International Universities Press, Inc., New York, Chap. 2, "Growth and Crises of the Healthy Personality," pp. 50–100.

NORMAL INDIVIDUAL TRANSACTIONS (Cont.)

INDIVIDUAL DEVELOPMENTAL AGE-SPECIFIC TASKS AND NEEDS	EXPECTABLE CRISES NATURAL, TRANSI- TIONAL AND PATHOLOGICAL	AVAILABLE INSTITUTIONS PROVIDING SERVICES
II. *Pre-school 3-6* *Tasks:* Initiative vs. guilt *Needs:* Learning, socialization, play	Child's separation from home, beginning resolution of parent-child ties Reaching out in the world Changing tasks of rearing *Typical Problems:* lack of preparation lack of supervision behavioral reactions	*Nursery School Recreational Centers* and see above
III. *Grade School 6-13* *Tasks:* Industry vs. inferiority *Needs:* Intellectual and social stimulation	Expanding world and increasing stimuli to be coped with *Typical Problems:* social and learning failures	*Grade School Activity* Groups and clubs and see above
IV. *High School 13-18* *Tasks:* Identity vs. identity diffusion *Needs:* Achievement and separation from parents	The time for decisions about sexual identity, work and the future *Typical Problems:* identity crises anomie addictions delinquency	*High School Employment* counseling services *Courts* and see above

NORMAL INDIVIDUAL TRANSACTIONS (Cont.)

INDIVIDUAL DEVELOPMENTAL AGE-SPECIFIC TASKS AND NEEDS	EXPECTABLE CRISES NATURAL, TRANSITIONAL AND PATHOLOGICAL	AVAILABLE INSTITUTIONS PROVIDING SERVICES
V. *Young Adult* *18-21* *Tasks:* Intimacy vs. self-absorption *Needs:* Opportunities for self-fulfillment in relationships	Leaving home Marriage Working *Typical Problems:* social failures anomie addictions crime	*College* and see above
VI. *Mature Adult* *21-65* *Tasks:* Generativity vs. stagnation *Needs:* Continuing opportunities for self-fulfillment	Household management and child care (refer as in a cycle to category I)	All of the above services
VII. *Aged Adult 65 and over* *Tasks:* Integrity vs. despair *Needs:* Living arrangements, physical care continuing opportunities for self-fulfillment	Physical and mental depletion Loss of friends and separation from family Death *Typical Problems:* sickness loneliness ennui	Some of the above services and institutional care services

This chart, being suggestive of a way to view individuals as they intersect with natural life crises and service provisions, has not included all of the unseen and possible need-meeting structures that are presently and potentially available in the urban society. In order that the reader's imagination might roam of its own accord, we might cite as well the following *locations* where all individuals go at some time in their lives, usually when they experience stress and strain, but increasingly because in the urban world, they need to rely upon their families or upon resources outside of themselves.

THE LOCATION OF SERVICES

We have already mentioned hospitals, clinics, and schools, as well as family and child welfare services and recreational centers. Outside of family and kinship groups, churches, and fraternal orders, there is a world of social structures that is literally integral to the individual's natural life-space as he conducts his life in the city of today. As a matter of fact hospitals and social agencies are most closely related to physical, social, and emotional breakdowns in human life; what of the structures that are related to health? Schools, neighborhood organizations, associations of professionals, civil servants and laborers, housing complexes, commercial establishments, parks and playgrounds, cultural institutions, and cemeteries, to name but a few of the locations where people *are* as they make their usual excursions through life. And, yet, the thrust of professional attention has been in those structures where people end up because these normal institutions of life somehow failed to meet their needs. Thus, institutions for the sick, the mentally ill, the penal offender, the neglected child, the neglected aged person appear to have overtaken those that are appropriately in the mainstream of life.

We have seen that social institutions have gradually become specialized in provision of services and meeting of needs of individuals in all stages of their lives and in all roles they enact. The family no longer is the locus of production, socialization, religious training, education, or authority, and it remains "structurally dependent on external systems, making it impossible for the family to exist as an entirely self-sufficient unit."[86] Yet, there is a primary function still left to families that, as far as can be seen presently, cannot be transferred satisfactorily to the society at large. "The family is emotionally intimate, and its historical duration for the individual is often greater than other groups; it is expected, in our society, to be the locus of emotional expression and emotional support for adults as well as for children."[87] This being true, there are streams in the organization of society that seek to protect the integrity of family life, if its primary purpose rests only in its provision of intimacy, affection, and generativity. It is important to note both the necessity and the limitations of family life, so as not to exaggerate either aspect. Family life functions have changed in the urban society; family life may not have broken down as much as it may have taken on a highly specialized burden of providing an arena for affection and intimacy. This requirement for all individuals must surely be of major concern to social institutions that seek to promote individuality for all urban citizens.

The post-industrial or technological era which we now confront is characterized by urban living and its inherent complexities and isolation. We see social institutions serving individuals in most aspects of their lives, many of them supportive of family life and others substituting for family life. As we have discussed, none of us is any longer capable of coping with our specialized needs in the urban society. As our chart has shown, from cradle to grave we intersect with society in informal and formal ways, and the transactions that occur thereby are systemic as individuals and institutions affect each other through feedback mechanisms.

Developmental services follow the present natural life style of the individual; they need not be confined to the

[86] Leichter, Hope Jensen and Mitchell, William E., *Kinship and Casework*, Russell Sage Foundation, New York, 1967, p. 27.

[87] *Ibid.*, p. 284.

pathologies with which we are familiar. Theoretically the entrance of social organizations in the lives of individuals will contribute to prevention of later breakdown of functioning of both the individual and society. Transactional relationships mean that the process of reform is not linear or one-directional; the existence of developmental services will not only provide necessary services for individuals but also will be a barometer of need in the community as individuals in a sense "inform" society of social breakdown and unmet need. Developmental services then are becoming the hallmark of the technological, urban society, and necessarily they will be highly bureaucratized agencies. The question will then confront us as to how these agencies can be drawn to the human scale and made accessible and responsive to individualized need. One way which we have mentioned earlier is through decentralization of services, making them, wherever possible, local and based in neighborhoods and defined communities. Thus, a day-care service might be in a neighborhood where families live, and a family casework service might be located in a downtown business area, accessible to working men and women. Further assuming that the strains of modern life are such that family problems are almost universal, family casework and family life education would, in this view, be a developmental service.

Social institutions which are essential to the conduct of urban life must be humanized. Individualizing social work services could facilitate the adaptation of urban life to the individual, so that he does not become overwhelmed by its impersonality.

As the foregoing chapters have indicated, it is our thesis that the urban society increasingly will need to provide institutional supports for all individual citizens. Some members of society are more able to cope with strain and crisis than others, either because they are more capable in some way, or because they have easier lives and more money and resources to cope with life; nevertheless, it seems increasingly apparent that urban strain is not to be confined to a particular class of people, nor to any ethnic group alone. Urban living—the condition of life for increasing millions of people in this country—is impartial; it has an impact upon everyone.

A second thesis that we have presented early in the book is that social work practice has gradually been failing in its primary mission which has been to provide individualized social services as they are needed. This failure may be attributed to overspecialization, to technical concentrations without significant meaning, to preoccupations with professional status, to undiscriminating borrowing from other disciplines, particularly medicine for its practice models and psychoanalysis for its practice theory, or in the case of community organization, politics as the practice model. One of the binds in which social workers find themselves is that the work they do best, the individualizing work in social welfare, is often thought by others to be done perhaps even as well or better by volunteers, neighbors, family members, the clergy, the family doctor, the bartender, the public health nurse, the teacher, by any professional something else, or by a well-meaning friendly person. If this is the actual image held of the social worker, then somewhere social work has not made explicit to the public what its expertise is. Here we are not talking about a mere public relations matter, but about the content and quality of the social worker's practice itself.

So we are faced with the picture of community need on the one hand, and a potentially relevant practice on the other hand. Our concern is to try to bring these two forces together. The city of today presents the highways and byways in the modern world, and it could well be the social work practitioner who will place himself at the crossroads, the points of intersection where individuals meet society. Perhaps it is not possible to identify as professional those actions that are undertaken to promote individuality in a society. Perhaps, as in less urbanized conditions, we might yearn for a more intimate role of the family, the neighborhood, the church, the friendly general practitioner or the town sage as the person who will best listen to our troubles and tell us where to go to make use of the community's resources. Undoubtedly, it would be pleasant to have back that world, but it is quite gone . . . as an urban condition, if indeed it ever existed in the idealized form. It is gone along with the sense of homogeneous community, quiet streets, clean air, absolute respect for authority, well-behaved youth, obedient Negroes, kitchen-bound wives and mothers, one-family houses, and horsedrawn carts. The do-it-yourself motif may be a reaction against the over-specialization of society, but if professionalized and human-ized help is available and can be demonstrated to be better than lay services, social work practice may help to fill the need felt in all of urban society.

THE LIMITATIONS OF INSTITUTIONAL SERVICES

The provision of human services by the public or private sector of a community may be an indicator of social responsibility or of social control, depending upon who is providing the services and toward what aim. For example, the study of civil disorders precipitated by pro-testing youth or blacks may be justified in the aim of pre-venting further bloodshed, or instead, of devising ways of containing future outbreaks. Services for delinquents, nar-cotic addicts or unmarried mothers also take on a different coloration when their fundamental aim is to control the outbreak of the problem rather than to actually give helpful attention to the person who suffers the problem. The anti-poverty war is a further example of two levels of motiva-tion for a program. Was its aim to saturate poverty-stricken communities with services and tools for change because people desperately need these, or was it instead a substitute of a program for a wrenching redistribution of the nation's financial resources? In effect, did the poverty program hold out a carrot to the poor? We have observed the necessity in the urban world for human services to be provided out-side of the family, in the community and through social institutions. Yet we cannot be assured that the public's institutions will prove to be lenient in their standards for human behavior, in their observation of individual privacy, or in providing really free alternatives for action. The intimacy of family life appropriately provides for secrets, for tantrums, for illogicalities and for halting steps toward development; its best purpose is to support uniqueness. Can we be assured that public or socially sanctioned voluntary agencies will truly provide for human differences and give people the freedom to be, or not to be? We have made our comment upon the inevitability of extrafamilial developmental and universal institutional services, and now we must work at its implications. For if we do not build-in individualizing protections, then we will run the risk of becoming an Orwellian society holding out a predefined mold of human being.

It is around the humanizing of services, the protection of the maximum amount of individuality in public provision of services, that our narrative of the problems of urban life intersects. We have spoken earlier of the sense of isolation and anomie, really the feeling of powerlessness, that seems to characterize our lives in the urban and technical society. We vote in elections and sometimes we work through political or social organizations hoping to promote interests we hold in common with others. More and more in our society we find less response from centralized government and bureaucratic service agencies; our problems and our sense of loss seem too diffuse to communicate and too vast for officials to cope with. Paul Ylvisaker has said, "Thanks to the Negro, we have developed a fourth branch of American government . . . the March."[88] Perhaps this form of demonstration of need is heard more than any other individual outcry. Surely the campus revolts and the protest at Chicago and the Watts rebellion accomplished social changes to a larger degree than would have been thought possible. But protest marches and demonstrations

[88] Ylvisaker, Paul, "Working Session on Centralization and Decentralization," *Toward The Year 2000, Daedalus,* Summer 1967, p. 682.

and rebellions and riots are potentially dangerous, both for
the people involved who may be hurt and for society at
large that may suffer from the ultimate and inevitable
police or military controls that always come in response to
incipient revolution. Is the sense of powerlessness to find
its expression in violence, or will it be possible to meet it
through the primary involvement of people in the institutions that are necessary for their survival in the urban
world?

Richard Goodwin, who has made some observations on
the current "large and serious revolutionary movement" in
this era, states:

> There is a serious discontent not only with what we as
> a nation are doing but with who is doing it. There is a
> challenge to the "power structure" itself, which means
> simply the methods, institutions, and people by which de-
> cisions affecting the public are made.[89]

The political rallying cries heard earlier in this century had
to do with substantive promises of a chicken in every pot
or a car in every garage, or the feeding of one third of the
nation. There was an understanding of the need for greater
beneficence on the part of agencies of government or private
enterprise which has presently given way to a popular
search for participation in the very decisions involved in
the allocation of goods and services. This is not to say that
goods and services are not essential to people and most
particularly to the poor; rather that the movement seems
to be directed toward changing the process of provision.
According to Goodwin, it is the sense of powerlessness in
this regard that is felt by all classes and is the "source of
the public's unhappiness."

It is perhaps a presumption and an oversimplification
to compare people's present frustration with being "given
to" without a chance to be involved in the terms of the
giving, with the old experience social workers had in giving

---

[89] Goodwin, Richard N., "Reflections: Sources of Public Unhappiness," *The New Yorker*, Jan. 4, 1969, p. 38.

Christmas baskets to the poor. Although this might have been a kind action and even a life-saving service for a family, in the end it might have been a source of anger to the family who was forced by circumstances into the compromising position of grateful recipient. Despite the fact that most goods and services today are not given through charity but are paid for in some fashion by the recipient and are not intended to be of the let-them-eat-cake variety, the role of passive recipient must be an uncomfortable one. Recalling that the human services are presently accepted as an important responsibility for government to provide for its citizens, they are increasingly those services that once were provided by the family. This public, institutionalized, and specialized provision of basic human, individualizing services has become an absolute requisite of modern urban living, and the protections of individuality and participation in important decisions are no longer present as they were when families were able to care for themselves and to take the primary role in the rearing of children and the transmission of culture.

The loss of intimacy that has accompanied the decline in influence of the family is matched by the anonymity and detachment of the technological age, making the need for meaningful participation in one's personal life even more important. The worker in a factory has no opportunity to develop a significant investment in his own work when he must deal with a mere fragment of the product being made. He may never know what value his skill serves, and he may never see the end product he has helped to create. The loss of connectedness is apparent in the case of the office worker, too, who has become the backbone of the organization world that could not run without computers, automatic typewriters, and Xerox machines. However, as buttons are pushed, the most skilled and highly trained office worker may never know the meanings of the input or the output. If all IBM cards look alike, what is the difference that one set counts stock transactions and the other heartbeats? The salesman, the designer, the manager, the technician all

develop generic skills having less and less need for reference to the particular purposes of the skills they perform.
The day does not seem too far distant when professionals,
too, will be relying upon machinery and electronic transla-
tions that will determine more effectively than the patient,
the client, or the student the nature of services needed.
Our civilization is faced with the need to return to all people
who are caught up in technological progress some access
to individuality and participation in the ordinary processes
of life.

The observation had been made over and over again
during the middle years of the 1960s, the years of social
outbreak, that *at least* black and student movements had
causes to pursue; the activity of protest has meaning in
and of itself, quite apart from the object of the protest.
This notion is reminiscent of the heightened expression of
human values during the Depression years and during the
London Blitz when people were kinder to each other under
the threat of a common problem. We know of the camarad-
erie and the excitement felt by those who march together,
sit in, or form communes. Yet, it would be an irrational
society that sought a continuing state of protest, demonstration, and rebellion—or war or depression—so that its citizens could experience a sense of meaningfulness and unity
through participation in "doing their own thing." The task
before us is somehow to humanize the necessarily organized
world so that people do not have to suffer the sense of re-
moteness and isolation from control of their own lives.

> A people suffering from institutions that can't respond,
> problems that are virtually left untouched, and the myriad
> uncertainties of their own private and public existence
> must inevitably rise in protest.[90]

So our traditional primary social institutions like the
family and the church, and the structures of another age,
like homogeneous neighborhoods, one-room school houses,
character-building youth organizations, and town meetings,

---

[90] *Ibid.*, p. 44.

have declined in their influence. In their stead have arisen bureaucratic monoliths, bigger and presumably better health, welfare, and education establishments and increasing codification of the way in which their services will be provided to the people. As professional expertise improves, knowledge, skill, and technique in the health, education, and welfare areas of urban life achieve fantastic heights. But it may be, ironically, that those achievements could hasten the decline of personal control. For the social distance is increasing rapidly between the efficient bureaucracy and the individual who must rely on it. The medical staff that is competent and self-confident is less likely to take the patient into the decision-making processes that concern the patient. Thus efficiency may in itself tend to isolate the patient from participation in his own life's decisions. We are not only concerned about the inefficiencies of bureaucratic organizations; in fact when they break down they are more likely to hear from their consumers than when they are operating on a high level of efficiency.

The dilemma is indeed one of institutional affluence, where a plethora of services, and most particularly good and expert services, could separate and isolate further the individual who is forced by the urban condition to rely upon institutions that are outside his control and jurisdiction. How can this distance be reduced so that humanization in urban terms will evolve as the hallmark of a democratic society?

Each person who seeks the solution to this most crucial problem of institutional affluence perceives the answer in his own terms of reference. Clearly it is a problem that must be attacked on all fronts at once; all approaches are locked together systematically; all rely upon each other for their potential effectiveness.

PROMOTION OF PARTICIPATION

We have assumed that all people in the urban society need to have, and not only to feel, a sense of participation in the forces and institutions that affect and control their lives. There is no simple prescription for this in a crowded, unplanned, and competitive urban environment, where the sources of goods and services are so remote from the citizen who must partake of them. So that we can see the total system of human services, those that provide for health, education, and welfare, it might help to break up the spectrum and view the components of the system separately. Here we are addressing the ways in which the service systems might be better able to provide for participation and involvement of the individual.

1. The primary function of *institutionalized human services*, of course, is the improvement of the quality of life through provision of adequate financial resources, housing, recreation, education, health care, transportation, access to the advantages of the city, and the beautification of the environment. If the general quality of our lives could be enhanced we would, of course, have less reliance upon residual service structures, and people undoubtedly would feel less unhappy about their lives in the city.

2. *Urban planning* would need to provide the physical possibility for the smallest possible units of health, education, welfare, housing, and recreational facilities. Housing projects, if only somewhat smaller, would reduce the span of management and provide for a degree of face-to-face contact for its tenants. Hospitals that had outreach health and clinical facilities spread through communities would be able to utilize the centralized facility for patient care and research rather than for family care. Schools dispersed throughout neighborhoods would give parents and teachers their opportunity to communicate and would provide for full community participation. Welfare offices and social agencies, if decentralized, would become part of the fabric of community life, as would all other requisite social institutions and would be more capable of providing services in accordance with the natural life style of the particular community groups they would serve. And should there not be within easy access in every community a library, park, day-care center, theater, and meeting hall? Although it may all sound unreal to even suggest such guidelines for urban

planning, it would be completely unreal to consider other humanizing aspects of urban life without reference to the physical planning that is interrelated.

3. *Bureaucratic organizations* must decentralize so that their services will be closer to the people, more visible, and accessible. Once they are localized they will, of course, come under greater influence of their constituency, whose members might serve in all instances as local policy makers, bridges between the agency and the people in the community, collectors of data, translators of need, and, increasingly, working participants in programs.

4. *Individualizing services* will be required to help people negotiate the complex service systems, to bring institutions and citizens together in their common task of provision for survival in the city, and to provide direct help to every person who wants and/or needs it. The nature of these services, the terms of their availability, their aims, and their methods ought to reflect the highest degree of community participation. These individualizing services, more than buildings, organizations, and policies, are the closest to the individual's own interest and would provide for his particular expression of himself. Just as a community board might participate with the administrators of the local hospital in determining the most convenient clinic hours, it would be possible for the community board to bring to the attention of the hospital the prevalence of a health problem that is showing itself in the neighborhood. Would it not be even more appropriate for this process to be invoked with social agencies as increasing numbers of recipients of service take their places on boards and advisory committees?

The *terms of service* are community issues and actually have little bearing upon the professional's expertise. Who is to be served, under what eligibility rules, for what purposes, and under what conditions are the terms that would best be decided by the people who would receive the services. This feedback process is being demanded by organized groups in the black, the poor, and the student communities, and although it might appear to be a threat to the professional doctor, lawyer, teacher, and social worker, who have all enjoyed rather total autonomy in assessing terms of service, this participating process can only support the professional services themselves. People have begun to recognize their need for participation in the remote urban institutions, and they will not wait too long before they insist upon it.

The implicit threat to professionals is of course similar to the threat of popular demand upon governments. Will the people "take over"? Will vested interests be exposed and exchanged? Will favored professional techniques and stances be challenged and found wanting? The risks are very real, but the alternatives are limited. In the first place, the primary purpose of professionalism is to serve the public, and the public of today in the urban world wants and needs to have something to say about the services it requires. Second, participation in the terms of service could enhance the use of the services by the public. Feedback to the institution by the consumer of information, of unmet need, of timing and coverage of services would engage people more purposefully in their own modes of help. This engagement could only improve the quality of help in instances where cases are found before too much damage has occurred, where clientele are helped into care by their neighbors, where professional experts are known by their patients, where people in the community can be called upon to provide supports for those who are in difficulty, where the lines of communication between person and organization are open, and where resentments are less likely to build. And a third reason for providing for this kind of participation in the terms of service has to do with the increasing complexity of causation of physical psychological and social problems; the multi-dimensional threads of causation and the unknown directions of social change seem no longer to be within the boundaries of any profession's capacity to understand or to solve. It would seem then, that the only way to remain in touch with the strains of social phenomena is to seek the feedback from the constituency that reflects those strains.

Thus, we reach for a new form of institutional services

to arise in the urban context. Perhaps this will happen before "the fire next time," so that unlike a Phoenix rising from the ashes, there will be a sophisticated, modern institutionalized response to the stifling, remote and debilitating urban condition.

We come then to the role of social work practice that must derive from such a view of the urban scene in the modern age. There will be, undoubtedly, an increasing role for the practitioner, and in the next section we will explore the implications of a methodology that would be utilitarian in the present fluid social situation. Participation by the public in the terms of service will create demands for relevant and expert professional practice; for an effective practice that can be identified as different from that which one's neighbor or psychiatrist or community leader can provide.

5

the process of individualization

> But society equalizes under all circumstances,
> and the victory of equality in the modern world
> is only the political and legal recognition of
> the fact that society has conquered the public
> realm, and that distinction and differences
> have become private matters of the individual.
>
> ——Hannah Arendt[91]

---

[91] Arendt, Hannah, *The Human Condition*, Doubleday Anchor Books, Garden City, 1958, p. 38.

WE HAVE TAKEN some pains in the foregoing chapters of this book to set the scene for the discussion of methodology in social work practice. By this time it should be evident that we do not see method as an entity, standing by itself without reference to what is going on in the world. *It must be reflective of the milieu in which it is practiced,* in our case, the urban milieu in crisis. Thus, it must account for the extremely fluid roles being enacted by urban citizens, for heightened tensions, for pressures that derive from discontents, and for participation of people in the terms of service that affect their intimate lives. *The aims of social work practice are probably more important to identify than its techniques,* because techniques used for obscure or irrelevant aims can serve no social purpose and sooner or later those techniques become endangered of being ends in themselves. We might suggest here that the primary aim of social work practice is to enable people to command their own lives and destinies to the greatest extent possible in light of the isolating, technological, specialized, and hopelessly complex world in which we live in the last half of the 20th century. In view of the fact that public institutions have gradually encroached upon personal functions and that publicly defined goods and services have compensated for each individual's inability to provide them for himself, an important part of commanding one's own life and destiny is the opportunity to be connected with those goods and services that are provided increasingly through impersonal organizations. Thus the aims of social work practice have to include ways of connecting people with goods and services, possibly by arranging pathways, promoting accessible organizations, and advocating and strengthening individuals to cope with the confusing array of urban structures and diffuse relationships that are symptomatic of the modern world.

Once having placed social work practice in a relevant social context, *its methods and techniques will only take on meaning when they are viewed within a recognizable framework.* In social work that framework is constructed of components of *knowledge* about individual, group, and organizational behavior, community structures, social institutions, social policy, and socio-cultural determinants, and the *skills* necessary to work in these areas of limitations. In addition to knowledge and skills, social work practice rests upon a set of *values* that guide its working principles and define the ways in which knowledge is used. These values have been described as traditional humanistic, Judeo-Christian values that include acceptance of people as individuals in their own right, respect for their differences and their integrity, and promotion of the social good. Without a framework surrounding practice activities, the methods and techniques used in social work would look like the work of individualizing that goes on in all human encounters. Neighbors talk with each other; ministers counsel their congregations; politicians listen to their constituencies; doctors sympathize with their patients while they care for their bodies; psychoanalysts treat people for their personal problems; and teachers, nurses, lawyers, psychologists, and bartenders, along with all other social and professional roles individualize their clients and their friends and relatives directly to be of help, or indirectly in the course of another, more primary activity.

Thus the explicit framework that defines social work practice is important to keep in mind, for the primary work of social work is individualizing, which is also the process that occurs formally and informally on all occasions, among all people. It is a continual challenge in discussing the purposes of social work to avoid underestimating and generalizing it as a process that everybody can use with the same effectiveness, or overestimating it as a singular solution to the strains of urban living. In truth, it is a practice that has grown through history as an organizational expression of society's interest in providing help to people. Through time, the concept of help has changed, as has the notion of what people are to be the objects of help and what aegis is to be the controlling agent of help. The practice of social work seems to have surpassed its original purposes, and it is time to look at its present-day functions which may yet prove to be more necessary and effective than they were in previous eras of our history.

Before examining the process of individualization that would have relevance for social work practice in the modern urban world, a word needs to be said about the *role of expertise*, for we have pointed out in earlier chapters some of the changes occurring in our society that are posing challenges to the once assumed clarity of the professional's functions. *Knowledge* of what is best for a client is no longer as sure as it once seemed, partly because the world is too complex to be thoroughly known by any professional discipline. The authority of knowledge is increasingly challenged by thinking young people and newly liberated minority groups in society who have viewed its structures afresh—and with alarm. A practice like social work, for example, also has had to confront squarely its limitations in solving basic economic problems or creating basic social change, and thus the usefulness of its expert knowledge may be suspect. Also expert knowledge is not necessarily a friend of political power struggles, and where politicalization of the nation's poor and minority group populations has become a sign of the present urban crisis, professional knowledge will have severe competition from power politics as the basis of human improvement. Finally the need for people to participate in the terms of service will inevitably impinge upon the arena of expertise that has been held up as one significant aspect of professional practice. We cannot discuss the expertness of social work practice in the process of individualization without taking these issues into consideration.

THE MEANING OF INDIVIDUALIZING

A primary characteristic of an individualizing process is to *differentiate* people, one from the other, to single them out from the mass. According to the *unit of attention* (about which we say more later) that a practitioner addresses, whether it be a person, a family, a group, or a community, individualizing terms have to be applied. Therefore, a *person* must be known by his identifying bio-psycho-social characteristics, his role and status in his immediate society, his interactions with those meaningful people around him, his modes of adaptation and of coping with his world, his strengths, and his problems. His uniqueness might differentiate him as a black person from all other blacks, even while his most significant reference group might be the black ghetto in which he lives. He might be poor, but he will survive in his state of poverty in his own life style, accommodating, angry, aspiring, or complacent. He might be mentally ill, delinquent, addicted to narcotics, or even well-adjusted in the society, stable, and earning an income; whatever his condition of life, we will know him as an individual only through understanding his very particular needs, feelings, desires, physical and mental characteristics, and style of life.

When a family, a group or a community is similarly individualized, it is known through its uniqueness, despite all that it holds in common with other like groups of people. This differentiation process is familiar to social caseworkers as *psycho-social diagnosis,* the "knowing through" or in Gordon Hamilton's terms, "understanding of the need or problem the client presents."[92] The first definition of psycho-social diagnosis was stated by Mary Richmond as "An exact a definition as possible of the social situation and personality of a given client."[93] According to Menninger, "diagnosis is not a label, but understanding for specific help."[94]

On the face of it, it would seem that diagnosis as a synonym for differentiation, designation, or distinguishing one from another class of objects should be a perfectly acceptable concept to serve an individualizing process as is practiced in social work. Yet it is one of the greatest areas of contention within the field of social work itself, and perhaps even about the field from nonsocial workers.

[92] Hamilton, *Op. cit.,* p. 214.

[93] Richmond, *Op. cit.,* p. 51.

[94] Menninger, Karl, *et al., The Vital Balance,* Viking Press, New York, 1963, p. 7.

It is important to ponder this phenomenon, that a utilitarian concept has somehow gone astray and become the scapegoat for social casework failures. Is it a utilitarian concept? What features seem not to sit well in the modern urban scene? Are there, perhaps, misunderstandings about its meanings, or misapplications of its primary purposes? Diagnosis, like any other practice concept, is a creature of its times. As a movable and responsive notion, it should undergo transformations in every era and reflect the socio-cultural, economic, and psychological determinants of the day. If it does not, then its usefulness is at an end; if there is a core of usefulness to the concept as it moves through history, then in each changing period it must be re-examined and re-evaluated in current terms.

We will look again at the diagnostic process itself and think about what can be retained and what might have to be changed. The *what* or the *object* of diagnosis has always changed through time, even if the how of it has remained the same. The *uses* to be made of it in treatment or in expanded forms of help have also changed in response to the changing scene, even though the purposes of the diagnostic process as a guide to treatment have remained the same. Assuming that diagnosis is an essential component of the individualizing process that must distinguish among people and the precursor of any kind of treatment, help, or service that is geared to the individual's requirement, we can explore its changing subject matter, the object it must address in these times, and its changing uses. We continue to perceive diagnosis as an important concept which needs only to be placed in the proper contexts of modern urban society and new knowledge.

MISCONCEPTIONS ABOUT DIAGNOSIS IN SOCIAL CASEWORK PRACTICE

Despite the lifelong efforts of Gordon Hamilton to demonstrate the contrary, diagnosis has a medical connotation. Useful as the concept may be to the social caseworker who has used it as a term of psycho-social assessment of the case, it is defined in the dictionary and thus by the public as: "Determination of a diseased condition; identification of a disease by investigation of its symptoms and history."[95] Perhaps it is the medical connotation that has given so much trouble through the years, for the dictionary definition unfortunately does confine the meaning to disease, symptoms, and history. When taken literally, instead of in the context of the theoretical translation made by Hamilton the dictionary definition does indeed place severe limitations upon the modern practitioner. According to Hamilton:

> Essentially, diagnosis is the worker's professional opinion as to the nature of the need or the problem which the client presents. It is not a "secret labeling of the client," it is not an uncontrolled adventure into the mysteries of life; it is a realistic, thoughtful, frank and "scientific" attempt to understand the client's present need, which is always a person-in-situation formulation, including interpersonal relationships.[96]

For example the medical term directs the social worker to pathology or psycho-social breakdown after the fact, as it were. Even Hamilton's concentration upon *what is the matter* presumes a problem status in the case. When we consider later the possibilities of broader boundaries of practice and ideas about earlier intervention in the status of a case, we will find that exclusive concentration upon pathology, problem, and "what is the matter" might prove to be excessively confining.

Another problem with the medical definition is that it leads one to seek *symptoms*, which of course serve as clues for the doctor or the psychoanalyst about the nature of the disease entity. The practice of social work is not analogous here for several reasons. In the first instance, the view of a psycho-social case includes social factors interacting with personal ones, and in the example of a malfunctioning poor

---

[95] Oxford Universal Dictionary, Third Revised Ed., Oxford University Press, London, 1955.

[96] Hamilton, *Op. cit.*, p. 214.

family living in deplorable slum housing conditions in a ghetto area of the city, it would be almost impossible to identify symptomatology unless one were to oversimplify the concept by stating that the society was diseased and poor housing was one of its symptoms. Although such a designation might give us a clue to the problem at hand, it would not lend itself to a classificatory scheme nor direct us to a treatment measure that was feasible for practice.

Second, the identification of medical symptoms is usually the end result of tedious clinical study; the eruption of a symptom has meaning only if it is known to belong to a category of like behaviors that have been observed clinically over time. In social work practice most of the work done is extra-clinical, and there is only beginning to be a research component built into services that would contribute to the categorization of symptoms. As the parameters of each case are so broad, including the person and all aspects of his life in society, the conceptual net would have to be large enough to catch all of the fragments of the case in order to place them in a classification system that would provide for comparison of other, equally large, case components.

Finally, classical symptomatology has become an outworn term for modern medicine, particularly for those specialties like public health, general practice, and psychoanalysis in the present era. As Menninger describes so well in his view of *The Vital Balance*,[97] symptoms are economic devices employed by the ego "in the maintenance of organismic equilibrium and integrity . . . though being helpful in this regard, they add to the total difficulties of adjustment." Thus, symptoms are not to be seen as signals alone, but rather as part of the state of being in which the individual finds himself; symptoms seen in ego terms need not necessarily be considered expressions of disease but, in Menninger's view, are adaptive mechanisms and part of the total life situation of the person. This view of symptom might lead us away from the medical model of diagnosis, because

---

[97] Menninger, *Op. cit.*, p. 171.

it need no longer be seen as an expression of disease but rather as a function of ego-adaptation and coping capacity.

The third part of the definition of diagnosis that has proved to be confining to social work practice is the requirement for *history.* It would follow in medical diagnosis that, presuming a diseased condition, it would be essential to understand whether the symptoms—the way in which the disease is known—were of long or short duration, so as to determine whether the disease state was chronic or acute. Also history would tell the doctor a great deal about the patient's characteristic ways of living and coping with his disease, and this knowledge would give the doctor some predictive help. Where the social caseworker has pursued history as the primary source of understanding of his client, he has done so as a proper course in light of the medical model he has followed. Although social casework might be criticized for borrowing this diagnostic model it ought to be praised for its integrity in borrowing it *in toto,* for piecemeal borrowing would have made the system theoretically inconsistent. As long as a practice is addressed to disease or problem, the expressions of symptoms are the primary way to identify the pathological state, and history would then be the chief tool for understanding the meaning of the symptoms in the total economy of the person's past and present physical and mental adjustment.

There is no question that knowledge of the history of a person's development would enrich the understanding of his life. Literature is peopled with biographies and autobiographies which explain historical events better than political analysis could ever do. Humanity is ever curious about how people got that way and what made them do what they did; this curiosity is undoubtedly one of the most salutory expressions of our humanity, for we seek to know our brothers and to comprehend them totally. The life history belongs as well to lovers who want to know each other, to children who need to know from their parents and grandparents about how it used to be and what their roots were, and to all professionals who can only understand the presenting complaint or condition of their clients when they can see the threads of their actions developing in the past. There is no endeavor that is not clarified through the knowing of history.

Obviously, as far as professional practice is concerned, limits have to be set upon the kind of history that is sought and the time back to which data must be traced. These limits are usually defined by the nature of the service being provided. Thus a school teacher would need to know a child's school record; a lawyer, the previous relevant behavior of his client; a doctor, the course of his patient's disease or state of health. In professional circles, different from the intimate associations where people know each other's past in order to become closely related to them, psychoanalysis is probably the prototype of history-taking in depth. This is because the treatment method is in itself a redrawing of the patient's history, his childhood viewed through mature eyes with the aim of releasing him from its grip upon his present life. It is this model of history-taking that was followed by social casework in those early days of learning about psychoanalytic theory.

In the history of social casework there have been efforts to displace this theoretical model in favor of one that would be more present-centered. Other models, albeit not diagnostic ones, were sought in *functionalism*[98] and in *problem-solving*[99] that emphasized the helping process itself, out of which, it was expected, would come sufficient understanding to offer help without reliance upon past history. It seems that the diagnostic emphasis upon pathology, symptoms, and history has become an anathema to those who would bring social work practice into the modern scene. In some quarters it would seem that, as if in reaction to the medical mode, some other practitioners in social work would seek no theoretical model at all, but would simply follow the client's own path without intruding upon him any degree

---

[98] Taft, *Op. cit.*

[99] Perlman, *Op. cit.*

of professionalized knowledge, for fear of intruding upon his pursuit of his own life.

Notwithstanding the criticisms of diagnosis, and the confusion of the process of *knowing or individualizing* a person with medical and particularly psychoanalytical diagnostic and treatment methods, it is the thesis of this book that respect for individualization *requires* diagnosing or knowing the person, the group or the community. Although we would also depart from the medical model, we will join earlier efforts to translate the concept of diagnosis, as a useful differentiating construct, into a present-day social work framework. This will mean that we must pay attention to the unit of attention, changing knowledge, a different use for diagnosis in the helping method, and newer ways of achieving it. The process is basic to individualization, but how it is employed will undoubtedly modify it.

THE UNIT OF ATTENTION

The object of psycho-social diagnosis, the "what" to which social work practice pays attention, undoubtedly will color the "how" of diagnosis and its aims. A convenient term for this object of diagnosis is the unit of attention. The choice of the unit of attention rests in several considerations, such as the consensus of the community and social work's own definitions about the particular aspects of life that are to be the social worker's turf. Although it must be granted that such decisions are seldom made rationally and that sometimes a public health nurse or a mental health worker might vie with a social worker for the opportunity of working with a particular client group or providing a special kind of program, in the marketplace where professional practices are pondered, tested, and traded, a general agreement usually evolves, at least about the broad boundaries of all professional practices. A state may license; a profession may set up internal guidelines; a community may demand certain services. However territorial imperatives become structured, health, education, and welfare services eventually are allocated along some generally agreed-upon lines. The basic factors that ought to determine the unit of attention for any practice are the knowledge, skill, and ability to do something about the object it addresses—to be effective in providing its assigned services.

In the field of social work, where the boundaries of practice are potentially as broad as social welfare and as narrow as psychotherapy, it is more difficult than in most professions to define the unit of attention. A definition derives from observed needs in the community, values held by the profession, the history of its past actions, and to a large extent, the base of knowledge and skills that would hold out the promise of effective service. However the definition is arrived at, it will ultimately express the purposes of social work practice; thus it is important to look carefully at the implications of various approaches to the unit of attention.

One way to define the unit of attention is to create problem classifications such as delinquency, child abuse, unmarried mothers, school drop-outs, interpersonal conflict, effects of mental illness. As fruitful as it would be to have a functional classification system of psycho-social problems,[100] the fact is that there is no universally accepted scheme yet in present use, and as all problems need to be subject to interdisciplinary services, such categorization would not really specify the specific units of attention that could be addressed by social work practice. Furthermore, definition by problem category would tend to confine practice to pathology and social breakdown and not to health or prevention.

Historically the unit of attention in social work has derived from modes of practice; thus social casework traditionally has focused its methods upon individuals and families, group work upon formal and informal groups, community organization upon community groups and processes.

---

[100] Finestone, Samuel, "Issues in Developing Diagnostic Classifications for Casework," *Casework Papers 1960,* National Conference of Social Welfare, 1960, pp. 139–154.

This division of labor increasingly has become untenable for a number of reasons. People actually live out many roles, sometimes all at the same time, as individuals in their families, groups, a variety of communities; as citizens of the world. It is no more useful, probably less so in social work, to individualize in accordance with a professional specialty than it is in medicine to view an individual as a set of limbs, a collection of organs, or a network of nerves. In assessing the individual and his condition of life, particularly the person who lives in a mobile urban society where the social context is ever changing, it has become quite impossible to address a single social status such as the individual *qua* individual, or the individual in his family, groups, or community and expect to encompass the reality of the total and systemic experience of that person.

A third way of conceptualizing the unit of attention is to address categories of people in a variety of statuses. In this approach one would not need, as in the first approach, to presume the presence of problem or pathology, nor would the object of attention need, as in the second approach, to be forced into a pre-existing practice mold that is defined by social work and not necessarily responsive to the requirements of the people to be served. Typical of the classification of statuses that would be the units of attention are the poor, certain ethnic groups, children, or working mothers. These statuses are not related to problem categories *per se*; they are reflective of the urban condition. As we noted in Chapters 3 and 4, the mere fact of having any of these statuses may be a "problem" to someone, particularly, for example, if one were black, poor and a working mother, but none of those statuses indicate individual breakdown, even though their "problem" characteristics are evident in light of the conditions created by society at large that provide so little in the way of social supports for people of these statuses. Yet defining the unit of attention so that emphasis in service is provided for a particular group of citizens selected out from the mass has certain drawbacks. The question of universalizing the unit of attention in social work vs. specifying certain groups to be given a high priority for service presents us with a major dilemma.

To *universalize* means, as Richard Titmuss says, to recognize that "diswelfare" occurs to all people. As we have noted, our modern urban society is in a state of near revolutionary change and all of the inhabitants of cities and megalopolises—which increasingly is almost everybody in this country—are subject to the strains of this crisis. Moreover, the problems of environment, social isolation, and impersonal bureaucratic institutions affect all citizens in some way or another, and it does not appear that social planning on a national basis will evolve quickly enough to mitigate the effects of these urban problems. To universalize means to assume the right to services as opposed to demonstration of need; it means that services would be made available before the articulation of problems, and services would thus become part of the fabric of society available to all in the same sense as other facilities. We noted earlier that Kahn has called this view of service delivery *developmental services* and has described these services as social utilities.[101] There are significant problems with universalizing services or devising a unit of attention that would encompass all vs. some people. Some people do not have equal access even to universalized opportunities, nor do they enjoy the use of their own private resources that would compensate for urban "diswelfare." If the unit of attention in social work practice were addressed to all people, the avoidance of priority approaches could lead to lack of services for those people who need them the most. This is one of the horns of the dilemma.

On the other hand, there are also issues to consider in formulating the unit of attention around *selective* statuses, where special attention is given to some people because of their greater need and their greater reliance upon public or extra-family social institutions. Titmuss has brought out real concerns about choosing this approach.[102] In selecting

---

[101] Kahn, *Op. cit.*

[102] Titmuss, *Op. cit.*

out of the whole those particularly deprived groups who would require priority attention, there would need to be some form of means test to define eligibility. Where then would one draw the line? Assuming the poor are to be the primary concern of social work practice, it would be an arbitrary designation to assert that those families with income under $3000 would be eligible, and those with income above ineligible. The need to draw some kind of line could force people into functional molds that would not necessarily suit their style or even accurately describe them. Another example might be mentally ill people, and here again one would need to determine the eligibility boundaries that would inevitably become rigid in order to maintain the focus of selectivity.

Despite the fact that this approach to defining the unit of attention would provide for priority attention to certain statuses of people in special need, it would be impossible, as Titmuss points out, to avoid the stigma of the status, the meaning of which could interfere with voluntary use and public support of services. This dilemma has confronted social work practice throughout its recent history and may account for some of the criticisms it has suffered. Practice is damned for focusing upon services to poor people and not solving the problem of poverty, and it is damned for universalizing its attention and thus avoiding primary attention in its practice to poor people.

There seems to be only one way out of this dilemma or double-bind situation, and that is to define the unit of attention in social work practice broadly enough to include all people who would make use of social work services, inclusive, and flexible enough to account for all categories of need, and open enough to respond to continually changing expressions of need. After all, a theory of practice cannot be tied to a single status of people, such as blacks or the poor, for example, because times will change and need will be different; the problems of deprivation will look different in other times, and the people who suffer from deprivation may be other minority groups or groups with newly defined problems.

Titmuss has summed up this approach as follows:

> In all the main spheres of need some structure of universalism is an essential pre-requisite to selective positive discrimination; it provides a general system of values and a sense of community; socially approved agencies for clients, patients and consumers, and also for the recruitment, training and deployment of staff at all levels; it sees welfare not as a burden, but as complementary and as an instrument of change, and finally, it allows positive discriminatory services to be provided as rights for categories of people and for classes of need in terms of priority social areas and other impersonal classifications.[103]

Once having taken a position that social work practice should include in its unit of attention all people, with provision for selective attention to those in greater need, the burden upon differentiation through a diagnostic or distinguishing process of assessment becomes even greater if social work practice is not to become a total abstraction that would be *about* the people to be served, rather than *with* them.

In order to specify the unit of attention in individualizing social work practice we will continue to call it a *case*, the unique, differentiating unit that separates a person from all others. It is important to note that we are not referring to any particular kind of case here but merely to the conceptualizing of the unit of attention. In other words although use of the case formulation is familiar to social caseworkers, in the present context we would also differentiate as cases those individuals in groups and communities that are addressed in individualizing terms by all social work practitioners. Although the notion of the case historically has been the unit of attention for all professional practices, its meanings have changed considerably as evolving values, skills, and knowledge changed the perspectives of the case. In social casework the boundaries of the case have expanded, from attention to intrapsychic conflict,

---

[103] *Ibid.,* p. 134.

to interactional functioning; from the person *in* his family seen in family-centered terms,[104] to the person *and* his family seen in transactional terms.[105] In other words, use of the case as the unit of attention does not condition the practitioner to become psychoanalytic, or medical, or legal. The concept of the case is a movable one; its boundaries will change with the times. In order to place it in modern urban dress, we must identify the new *knowledge components* that are relevant to understanding that case, *adapt the process of individualizing* the case to the present social context, and adjust our conception *of aims of practice* with the case that will be consonant with the state of knowledge, the availability of skilled personnel and the urban reality.

THE BOUNDARIES OF THE CASE

The lens through which one would look at a case should be fashioned by the social context of that case. In the urban situation where people are wedged together in all degrees of congestion and where they must be reliant upon each other and upon services in order to survive, the view of the case would need to be through a broad lens, so as to encompass all of the essential elements. A *linear* view of man carries with it a certain nostalgia, of self-reliance, individuality, and privacy. Who would not wish to return to the era in this country, where people could determine the boundaries of their own existence, shape their own opportunities, and pursue obtainable goals? Of course the frontier myth was applicable only to certain people, but Social Darwinism kept the myth alive. It was thought that one could control his life and survive through being fittest, but even though the field of attainment was more open before the 20th century, in fact most people did not have

---

[104] Scherz, Frances H., "What is Family-Centered Casework?" *Social Casework,* October 1953.

[105] Spiegel, John P., and Kluckhorn, Florence, *Integration and Conflict in Family Behavior,* Group for the Advancement of Psychiatry Report, No. 27, August 1954.

access to the field of opportunities or they were not born equal. It does not seem possible today to approach "a case" as if it were independent of the circumstances of life surrounding it. There is no person of any class in the urban scene who can manage his own life without reliance upon others or upon formal organizations. Thus, to view the case through a linear lens, as if man were a self-sufficient being who could be understood in a straight line, as it were, is a kind of hopeless confrontation of reality.

Our lens would shed greater light upon our understanding of the case if it had an *interactional* prism, where it would illuminate the actions of individuals upon each other. Granting our assumption that people in the urban society are locked together, willingly or not, in their sometimes opposing efforts at survival, the view of a case would need to make provision for perceiving the many sides of the interactional processes and the actors in the scene. This broader lens would suit our purposes better than the first kind, for it would bring into focus a case of at least dual components, reflecting the interdependence of individuals in their multiple roles. Thus, such a lens would not define a case as being a man, a woman, and a child, or even a family unit, but rather a man as husband, father, or wage earner in *relationship* to a woman as wife, mother, wage earner, or homemaker, and also to children serving their function of the family as sons and daughters, and as students. The interactional threads binding all of these individuals to each other would be observed and lend themselves to description. In recent years theory of behavior has been enhanced by conceptualizations of certain interactional processes, such as the double-bind,[106] complementarity,[107] schism and skew,[108] and pseudomutuality.[109] So the inter-

---

[106] Bateson, G., Jackson, D., Haley, J., and Weakland, J., "Toward a Theory of Schizophrenia," *Behavioral Science,* 1956, Vol. 1, pp. 251–264.

[107] Meyer, Carol H., "Quest for a Broader Base For Family Diagnosis," *Social Casework,* July 1959.

[108] Lidz, T., Cornelison, Alice, Fleck, S., and Terry, Dorothy, "The

actional lens encompasses individuals in their many social roles that define their relationships in family, work, school, play, and all other social activities; moreover, viewing a case through this lens makes it possible to identify the processes that connect people, thereby opening opportunities for more precise intervention when relationships falter.

An interactional lens, however, is still too narrow in its scope when it is focused on individuals in their varied roles and relationships, for our perception of the urban condition suggests that there are other "actors" affecting all human experience, "actors" who may not even be in the relationship sphere of the individual in question but yet affect his life, "actors" that take the form of organizations which have become intimately connected in the life style of every individual in the urban society.

In order to grasp the meanings of these multiple elements in every case, one needs to change to a *transactional* lens so as to comprehend the influences that literally cross over the individual, affect him, and are affected by him. The notion of transaction suggests multidimensional interactions all in interplay with each other. A transactional view of "the case" does not mean a mere addition of components, but rather a reconceptualization of them, so as to be able to view a *system* of interweaving forces, all having reciprocity and feedback with each other. Before we look into a scheme for dealing with these multiple threads in every "case," we should take note of the widened parameters of the case that are suggested by this transactional view. We are now talking about the substance of the diagnostic or individualizing process; the *object* of the process.

The "case" boundaries would include the individual in his several social roles, interacting with his intimate rela-

Interfamilial Environment of the Schizophrenic Patient: II. Marital Schism and Marital Skew," *Am. J. Psychiatry*, 1957, Vol. 114, pp. 241–248.

[109] Wynne, L., Ryckoff, I., Day, Juliana and Hirsch, S., "Pseudo-Mutuality in the Family Relations of Schizophrenics," *Psychiatry*, 1958, Vol. 21, pp. 205–220.

tionships, usually his family, but *in addition* the dynamic environment of which he is a part. This would, differentially, include his extended family and diffuse relationships, his place of work, the schools his children attend, the neighborhood in which he lives, and the social, political, and commercial institutions that intersect his life. Moreover, the case boundaries would encompass his affiliations to culture, ethnicity, class, and specific value orientations. In the event that the individual has formal connections with a social agency, the agency itself would be a component of the dynamic, affective environment and thus also be viewed as "an object or instrument of change, rather than a given."[110] Clearly, the breadth and complexity of "the case" viewed through a transactional lens is going to require the use of vast amounts of knowledge, which must also be put together in some convenient way for the practitioner's use. The unit of attention in social work is *the case,* but it has very wide boundaries that have to be comprehended. First we need to find an organizing approach for the requisite multiple theories, then we need to identify the primary knowledge areas, and finally we need to place the whole individualizing process in a context of intervention. We must see how it would work in practice.

"THE CASE" AS A SYSTEM

General systems theory makes possible an organized view of the individual in his multiple interactions; it provides a convenient form for viewing the parts of things in an interrelated way so as to avoid fragmentation and disparateness. Menninger has commented on the part-whole question by differentiating the molecular point of view which assumes an entity to be invaded, from an atomistic or holistic point of view, where one sees "the totality of a living organism . . . not as the product of addition of parts, but as a unit within which parts may evolve *only by a delib-*

---

[110] Germaine, Carel, "Social Study: Past and Future," *Social Casework,* July 1968.

erate and temporary shift of focus on the part of the observer."[111] Keeping in mind that general systems theory is actually a theory about systems, a framework, and not in itself a substantive theory, it can be applied to many subjects ranging from space trips to the moon, to inventory measures used in industry, to the social work case. Boulding says of general systems theory that it is:

> . . . the skeleton of science in the sense that it aims to provide a framework or structure of systems on which to hang the flesh and blood of particular disciplines and particular subject matters in an orderly and coherent corpus of knowledge. It is also, however, something of a skeleton in a cupboard—the cupboard in this case being the unwillingness of science to admit the very low level of its successes in systematization, and its tendency to shut the door on problems and subject matters which do not fit easily into simple mechanical schemes.[112]

The theory has so many attractive possibilities as a scheme for organizing knowledge and as a framework for action that one must be careful to avoid overdetermining its value and thus ironically creating a closed system of the theory itself. An example of this can be found in *Reductionism*; the result of forcing of one system of ideas into a mold that would fit another system that is, in fact, unlike it. The danger in this is that neither set of systems maintains its own integrity, especially when one is a theory of apples and the other a theory of oranges. Reductionism could obstruct us from advancing our view of the transactions of the individual in his sphere of society. An example given by Reinhard Bendix suggests that "If the symbols of a culture are taken as a clue to the characteristic personality types of its participants, then we underestimate the incongruity between institutions, culture patterns and the psy-

[111] Menninger, *Op. cit.*, p. 90.

[112] Boulding, Kenneth E., "General Systems Theory—The Skeleton of Science," *Modern Systems Research for the Behavioral Scientist,* ed. Walter Buckley, Aldine Publishing Co., Chicago, 1968, p. 3.

chological habitus of a people, and we ignore an important part of social change."[113]

The accepted traditional social casework view of the *person-in-situation* illustrates the problem of separatism between social and psychological sciences. This concept requires the connectives *in* or *and*, because both the person and the (social) situation have different theoretical components and are actually measured by completely different yardsticks. The sciences of psychology and sociology are conceived on different levels of abstraction and point toward different levels of intervention, and the state of knowledge is such that to compress both kinds of knowledge into one would either psychologize society or sociologize personality. Thus, while keeping both sets of knowledge systems separate and intact, our task is to intertwine the useful person-in-situation concept in such a way that the hyphen is no longer needed. Through a systems conceptualization, we might be able to view person-in-situation as a transactional or *field* construct rather than as we have been accustomed to viewing it in linear or interactional terms. If it were possible (and of course it is not) to capture the essence of all possible theories about everything related to human behavior, sociocultural factors, social organizations, social planning, and method itself, it would be more than ever necessary to apply a systemic approach to the use of all that knowledge.

A conceptual umbrella is necessary to sustain a transactional view of a case, for without the reworking of the *organization* of ideas, one would be left with a lot of unparallel and disconnected meanings about concurrent happenings in every case. It would not take long for a practitioner to develop an affection for a favored theory; this has proved so in social work practice for fifty years as the pendulum has swung between inner and outer emphasis, even though the underlying concept has remained the person-in-situa-

---

[113] Bendix, Reinhard, "Personality Reductionism," *Personality and Social Systems,* Smelser, N. J. and Smelser, William T., John Wiley & Sons, New York, 1963, p. 61.

tion. In a systemic view there is no inner or outer, but rather an operational field in which all elements intersect and affect each other. John Spiegel comments on this problem of the common arrangement of data in linear form, making it almost mandatory to assign a hierarchy among levels of data. The familiar illustration in the social casework study would be the description of a case as one where a working mother who was clinically diagnosed as an hysterical personality had no plans for the day care of her children, and the case worker, while noting all of these components in the case, might seize upon the clinical manifestations and overlook the social problem of the need for day care. Spiegel writes:

> One handicap of linear hierarchy is that by focussing at one level then everything else becomes environment. We focus at points of interaction and neglect those interactions taking place in the extended field over time.[114]

By viewing our little case illustration transactionally, with the process going in all directions and reverberating back again, having modified all of the components, the case then becomes one of a working mother with clinical manifestations of hysteria whose children need day care which may not be available in the terms of her need, because her relatives are not available to care for the children, because of the neglected neighborhood in which she lives, or because of the child care system in the city which allocates services along nonfunctional lines. Furthermore, the mother's need to work might stem from her lack of money that would potentially connect her with the welfare system, with her husband's lack of support which could involve the family court system, or with her wish to get into the working world, which would connect her with the employment situation, or with her deep psychological push to avoid intimate relationships with her husband which might lead her toward

[114] Spiegel, John P., "A Model for Relationships Among Systems," *Toward a Unified Theory of Human Behavior*, Grinker, Roy R., Basic Books, New York, 1956, p. 17.

the social agency or mental health systems in the community. Whatever the diagnosis of the case, the parameters for study, diagnosis, and intervention are broader than the mother and her child, and causation may be identified in any or all parts of the field of the case.

As the family's situation has implications for the delivery systems in the community, so indeed does the set of service systems reflect back and affect the structure and function and adaptation of the family. As Spiegel would say, these are all field phenomena; they are not hierarchical or linear, nor do they necessarily derive from each other. They intersect at various points in the existence of all of the factors—the mother, her children, her husband, relatives, the institutions involved—and the balance of forces. Viewing a case in these terms makes it difficult to determine where one set of conditions begins and another leaves off, for they are in circular motion with each other; all depend upon the others for functional survival. When seen in this transactional state, they make the case for the social work practitioner who might intervene at any salient juncture and make a difference in the lives of the individuals involved. The vast opportunities for intervention in such a broad-scale view of the case will have significant impact upon changing social work practices and the use of non-professional manpower.

General systems theory is in a stage of rapid development. Its characteristics are changing as more is known about it, as new fields become interested and theoreticians try to make new applications of it. The reader is referred to source materials[115] here for a comprehensive understand-

[115] Katz, Daniel and Kahn, Robert L., *The Social Psychology of Organizations*, John Wiley & Sons, New York, 1966.

Parsons, Talcott, *Social Structure and Personality*, Free Press of Glencoe, Ill., 1964.

Smelser and Smelser, *Op. cit.*

von Bertalanffy, Ludwig, *General Systems Theory, System, Change and Conflict*, N. J. Demerath III and Richard A. Peterson, eds., Free Press, New York, 1967, pp. 115–129.

ing of the theory itself, for in the context of this book, our purpose is merely to provide tools of conceptualization for social work practice in the urban scene and thus to show how systems theory can be helpful. It would be a long detour to present a thorough exposition of systems theory in these pages. We continue to refer here to the social work case as a system and not to social work methods, which, of course, have their own systems characteristics. We will illustrate some of the systems concepts with another kind of case example, because the level of abstraction is still quite high in this theory, and examining the concepts through a typical case should make them more meaningful.

A three-year-old Negro boy is admitted to a general hospital in a ghetto area of the city for severe and extensive burns from lye. He sustained the burns as a result of coming between his parents when they were having a fight, and the mother threw the first available weapon at her husband. The weapon was a bowl of lye that was on the kitchen table.

The child must remain in the hospital for several months during which he has to undergo skin transplants and a series of other complicated medical and surgical procedures. Thus, in the language of the hospital he is a patient of pediatric, medical, and surgical services, and probably of several other categories of care, like a burn clinic, an orthopedic clinic, a skin clinic, an eye clinic, and a urology clinic. Moreover, he is known and visited regularly by a social worker, a psychiatrist, a psychologist, the whole range of doctors in all specialties and of all ranks, nurses, nurses aides, attendants, housekeepers, and volunteers.

His family consists of his mother, aged 19, his father, aged 22, and a baby sister aged 1 and a half. The mother's parents and brothers live in the South, and she has no present contact with them. The father has a mother who lives in a neighboring community and is the sole wage earner for her three children; her older children have left home either to be married or to go into the army.

The little patient's own family lives in substandard housing, an old slum railroad apartment divided into three rooms that all open into each other. Toilet and kitchen facilities are limited, the house is dirty, and the rent is too high for either the value of the apartment or the income of the family.

The mother had dropped out of high school in her junior year when she became pregnant at 16 with her first child, and the birth of the second child continued to keep her confined to her home. She wanted to return to high school but never quite knew how to arrange it, and she had no skills to do any kind of part-time work that was worthwhile to her. Her vocational aim is to be an office worker, and while she is intelligent, she has no skills that would make this possible. The father is a high school graduate, having worked to support his family at an auto repair shop. He became interested in advancing to a mechanic's status and took advantage of an OEO program to get involved in job training. At the time of the fight, when the child was burned, the father had just received a certificate that would qualify him for a better job in a large automobile service station.

The history of the marriage indicated a rather good relationship between the couple; they had a romantic attachment and had interests in common in their social outlets and in the children. The major source of irritation had been the mother's inability to go back to school or to work; she felt herself to be too young to be confined to her house all day, and she expressed her resentment to her husband and to the children in many ways.

While little is known of the family backgrounds of the boy, it is understood that they grew up in stable families, although neither of them had fathers at home. The wife's father had died when she was very young, and the husband couldn't remember ever having had a father living at home. Her background was southern and rural, and his was northern and urban. Neither of them had been particularly militant about political issues until the death of Dr. King, at which time they both became interested in a local movement to support Black Power in the ghetto and in the community at large. One of the wife's discontents was that her husband was out in the workaday world and could make contacts in the movement, and she was unable to do so as easily. Both parents appeared to be well-functioning, although the wife seemed to have a depressive quality about her. The husband has a more devil-may-care attitude and did not worry as much as his wife. Their fight was actually no more intense than any other argument they had, except for the crucial fact that she threw the lye in the heat of argument. Generally, they did not do violence to each other, but the lye was there, and she threw it.

It is assumed in systems theory that systems are either *closed* or *open*. To be closed means that components are self-contained and not dependent upon their surroundings for survival. To be open means that, as in the case of all living organisms, there is an *exchange* of energy between one system and another, between the element and its environment. There are no examples of closed systems in life, as plants, animals, and minerals all take something from their environment, utilize it for their own growth and then return some substance that has been modified by the exchange back into the environment. When social organizations, personalities, and relationships are viewed as systems, they can be described by the characteristics of open systems, for they must be mutually dependent upon each other for "survival." Yet it is not uncommon in viewing social systems that we find some that tend to be closed and end in a state of disintegration. When social systems are conceptualized as closed, they are not following a life model and, in a sense, are doomed as far as continuation is concerned. We all know of theories that are closed insofar as being responsive to new knowledge is concerned; in such cases, the theory, although a perfect entity, becomes dysfunctional in light of the new knowledge, and it finally is put to rest. The theory that the earth was flat could not survive in the face of evidence that the earth was round, and since the absolutism of the flat theory did not provide for the new information of vanishing horizons, it finally achieved a state of entropy. We know of small societies, where the sexes were kept separate and children were not born to replenish the society, that achieved a state of entropy as the elders died. By not letting in new influences, they could not generate a continuing society and thus became extinct. The matter of boundaries is important for our understanding of closed and open systems. Where the parameters of one system—whether broad or narrow—are too rigid and locked against intrusion from another system, the entity will not be viable.

Recalling our case illustration, there are several social systems operating all at once, and as we said that general systems theory provides a tool for conceptualizing and is itself not a substantive theory, we will do no damage to the boundaries of any of the operational theories by viewing the case systemically.

We see at once a set of *personality systems* that in this case are relevantly the boy in the hospital, his parents, and his baby sister. We view them as interacting and bound together through the common strands of their *family system,* and the permutation between these two systems makes both of them open and reliant upon each other. They would appear closed if we were to look at the child, for example, in a linear way, assuming that he was only a conglomerate of instincts and attitudes that had no bearing upon his family, or no responsiveness to their influences. Further, we see a *hospital system* and its many subsystems in the specializations represented by the many personnel we have mentioned. A continuing exchange of energy or influence among hospital, child, and family would characterize an open system, although we often find some examples of efforts at closure creeping into hospital organizations. Of course when closure occurs, it affects the interactional consequences. For example, the matter of visiting hours can be used to confine the hospital's activities and stiffen its systemic boundaries, or visiting hours could be used as an opening wedge for the family and hospital systems to interchange with each other and keep both systems open. Another example that would have bearing upon the openness of communications between the family and hospital systems is often found in the kind of medical information that is provided by the staff to the family or patient. Where the patient is kept out of the planning for his care and treatment, the hospital maintains closed boundaries which could affect the patient's improvement. Furthermore, where the hospital is not responsive to the patient's complaints about his care, there is less hope that appropriate changes will take place in the hospital system at large. We see that one system relies upon another for sustenance, and only as its boundaries remain permeable can we expect the system to stay alive and open.

As far as the parents are concerned, one might take a psychogenic or developmental view of them as having suffered familial and economic disadvantages themselves which could explain their marital conflict. On the other hand, one could also seek causation in the environment and in this case find that the husband's recent affiliation with a job-training program had secured his vocational future at the same time as the wife was feeling the pressure of rearing two small children in the face of her career disappointments. The notion that "energy" or causation can be identified in environmental systems, as well as within personality systems is well provided for in a systems framework. (We will see later, in Chapter 6, the expanded treatment possibilities that derive from using the systems framework in diagnosis.)

In the *feedback process* where energy is imported into the system, the theory accounts for the effect upon the system of the new source of energy, where the existing status of the system becomes transformed through the transactions of the person-family-environmental systems. In our case example we could identify the change of self-image experienced by the father when he sees the possibility of becoming a mechanic. Recalling that this is a black family that is apparently conscious of its black identity, their association with community organizations would undoubtedly contribute to a change of self-image for them all, creating hope for a better standard of living, and possibly playing a part in the wife's sense of impatience about not being able to work. The resultant marital conflict or the fight that resulted in the little boy's having been burned by the lye might also be understood as a reverberation of similar factors. According to the narrative of the case, although we do not know exactly what triggered the fight, we can now assume that the marital tensions were partially responsive to the changes in the husband's vocational status and the rising sense of expectations the couple were experiencing. One could cite the use of the lye in systems terms, by commenting upon the poverty subculture in the ghetto, where lye is a requirement to cope with insects and rodents and, as a reflection of that way of life, lye that is available in a bowl on the kitchen table becomes the poor man's weapon in domestic violence.

The *feedback process* operates not only within systems but also *among them in cyclical fashion.* In other words, after the lye-throwing incident, the private fight between the marital partners has become a public matter because the child has been burned, and the hospital has had to become involved in the family's activities and relationships. This provides the potential for "reworking" the interpersonal relationships and "returning" them improved, as it were, to the family system. The very fact of the publication of their fight makes possible the intervention of social service or psychiatric care or the provision of day care services, so that the wife might also go to work, or whatever treatment action that is seen to be relevant to the case assessment.

Where a state of tension occurs wtihin the system, the only way in which this tension can be expressed and thus subside is through environmental reciprocation and reinforcement. Using our case again, we note the family's participation in community processes which in turn contribute to the family's improved sense of dignity as black people in a hostile environment. Frustration occurs when the family's improved sense of dignity propels them into wanting greater participation in the benefits of society at large, and unless the world of work and money and housing responds appropriately and relevantly, the tension will build and create even greater frustration and discontent if it is not relieved in the system at large.

A dynamic balance is achieved when the system is in a steady state—when it is in motion but retains its original characteristics. In our case illustration we can assume that the marital relationship has proved to be workable for the couple, although it has been set off-balance at a time of marital crisis that seems to have been precipitated by the new job opportunity. If the complementarity between the marital partners is to be sustained, it will either occur by itself and they will "right themselves" through their own natural style of functional adaptations, or they may require some kind of professional help. In order to maintain their complementarity, or previous homeostatic balance, treatment will have to take into consideration the couple's tolerance for each other's job advancement, for example.

Another example in this case of the homeostatic principle that would govern treatment or explain the case might be seen in the absence of the boy from the family while he is in the hospital. As he is an integral part of the family system and serves a significant function, exemplified by his coming between his parents during their fight, his confinement to the hospital will require that his parents make some accommodation, alone or with help, to right their family balance. Assessment of ensuing imbalance would have implications for the hospital's flexibility in providing for family visiting, etc.

Assuming that the parents in our case would want to be more compatible about the question of their job competition, as well to live better in the society, the paths to these goals are multiple. Depending upon the diagnostic assessment, the kind of family situation it is and the kinds of systems with which it interacts, a range of approaches to these parents' accomplishment of their aims for themselves are possible theoretically. Beginning from "the inside out," the parents could undergo psychoanalysis and attempt to resolve their basic personality maladaptations; they could have marital counseling through a family agency; the wife could be helped to return to high school, so that she could go back to work; or day care services could be made available, so that she could return to work or to community action activities. As far as the child in the hospital is concerned, he could be treated medically only, or he could participate in ward activities to counteract the onset of "hospitalism"; visiting hours could be expanded to make possible his father's visiting around his working hours and his mother's visiting whenever she felt able to do so; a social worker could be available to see his parents when they visited; and the total range of hospital personnel could be engaged to provide for him a milieu of a health-promoting atmosphere. One, or all of these interventive modes, would derive from the systems framework. A simple picture follows of the systemic relationships between the family in our case example and the social systems in their transactional field:

Hospital

Medical
Institutional
and
Para-medical
Social work staff
and services

their individual personalities
their interactions
their family culture
their class, ethnicity, status
and role
their ego-adaptiveness
their family life style

FAMILY

Father . . . Mother
Son
Baby

School

Ghetto Neighborhood

Housing
Community action groups
OEO job training

Vocational school for father
High school for mother
Day care for baby
Headstart for boy

We have said that these are the relevant and transacting systems in the case. Assuming their concurrent influences upon each other, then intervention, wherever it occurs, will have a feedback effect upon another part of the system. The "case" has become a system of related factors; the diagnosis has expanded to include the systems related to the individual; interventive tasks can be located in any part of the case for these will effect other parts. The individual or the institution becomes "the client," because appropriate attention to either theoretically will enhance or at least affect the functioning of all.

CHANGING AREAS OF KNOWLEDGE

We have noted that the process of individualization can derive from a systemic view of "the case" and that the social work case in point has boundaries that are larger than the person. Clearly, the knowledge areas necessary for a practitioner are vast; they extend to whatever is salient for a particular individual situation. Thus a person who is an addict-client will require of his social worker that he have *substantive knowledge* about drug addiction, and the same can be said of unmarried mothers, neglected children, marital partners in conflict, welfare rights groups, etc. But weighty though these intellectual demands are, and difficult as it may be to keep up with the ever-changing substantive knowledge about people in urban life, there is yet more that needs to be known by a social worker in order that he practice wisely. In the diagnostic or assessment process, the conceptualization of a case in systemic terms requires a *knowledge repertoire of individual, group, organizational, and community processes,* all of which occur simultaneously over time in every case. Furthermore, as the case boundary is as broad as the individual's life style warrants, a practitioner has to have a working knowledge of *social policy,* both in order to know its impact upon the case, and to use his professional efforts to affect it and keep it relevant to changing conditions. This is why it is limiting to stay within the confines of social casework, for the boundaries of "a case" are social-work field boundaries, and they call upon all methods in social work.

Historically, social work has drawn upon theories of dynamic psychology and psychoanalysis, in particular, for its knowledge of personality development and behavior. In different eras, sociology, anthropology, political science, economics, law, and medicine have served as theoretical resources for social work. As society has pressed its demands for different social arrangements, as research has turned up new connections, so knowledge itself has changed. There is an inevitable lag in all professions when it comes to keeping up with new knowledge, partly because in the period when the professional student is in school he tends to be taught the content that derives from an earlier period. Unless professional education succeeds in teaching students how to keep their minds open, the next generation of students will, of course, perpetuate the lag by remaining wedded to older and perhaps outdated knowledge. A corrective in professional education for this lag rests in a freeing pedagogical method; in professional practice, it rests in devising a sufficiently *open methodological system* so that feedback of knowledge contributes toward a state of negative entropy and a state of equifinality. Only to the degree that new knowledge can find its way into a professional practice (input), to be acted upon (throughput) and applied relevantly (output) will that practice remain appropriate in the ever-changing society.

What kind of theory of behavior is essential for the social worker to practice?

1. Assuming that social work practice must attend to what is happening in urban life, in the streets and where people are, a theory of behavior would need to be one that explains how most people develop and cope with their lives —in other words, a theory of "normal" behavior.

2. Assuming that urban strain and limitations in the environment make it difficult for so many people to develop their potential fully, so that they fail to cope successfully

with their lives, the behavioral theory would need to explain as well the continuum from health to illness, from ability to cope to failure to cope with life.

3. Assuming that the function of social work is to help individuals in their many roles make an adaptation to their lives and find a sense of fulfillment, the behavioral theory would need to identify external, as well as internal mechanisms of adaptation, so that they are recognizable.

4. Assuming that social work practice is to be addressed to effective balance between individuals and the social institutions they inhabit and not to basic personality change, the theory of behavior must have an equilibriating component that will explain the balance of inner and outer forces between the person and his environment. Whatever the theory, it cannot be merely descriptive, static, or closed as a system; it has to be made applicable to the natural life style of individuals, which changes over time and across subcultures. An appropriate behavioral theory is that which is open to new knowledge as it occurs and is applicable to varieties of behaviors, and is also within the boundaries of professional expertise to know it well. Briefly, a useful theory should be relevant to the practice that makes use of it.

There are, of course, uncounted theories of how and why people behave as they do, if we assume that human behavior is more than the existential encounter. The theories range from religious ideas about spirituality to scientific behavioristic notions that would computerize actions toward understanding and control. In between these extremes are the range of theories that are based upon the basic social structure of the family and the development of children in this structure. Although there are variations upon the Freudian theory of human behavior, the idea that people are what they are because of what has happened to them in their growing up is the common 20th century conception of human behavior. Freud's discovery of the vast repressed area of the unconscious has colored the discoveries of social and behavioral scientists in this century.

There are many levels on which one can use this theory, and in social work practice, it has been a pivotal theory that has explained personality development. Unquestionably, one might argue for or against this theory or any number of orthodox or eclectic uses of it, but the fact remains that a characteristic of any professional practice is that one needs some theory from which to depart. This differs from the academic pursuit, where one may ponder the contributions of any and all theories, in order to develop a theory of theories or even to merely enjoy reveling in the likenesses and differences of various theories. Such knowledge, in academic pursuits, can become an end in itself; but a practice requires theoretical tools, so that the practitioner of whatever discipline will bring a frame of reference to the situation which he addresses. Therefore, we must forego the intellectual luxury of contemplating uncounted explanations of any human actions. In order to act in a disciplined and professional way, we must finally select a theory or a set of compatible theories, so that we can get on with our work.

The thesis in this book is that Freudian theory, which attempts to explain developmental determinants and personality structure, is a useful theory that has had acceptance and demonstrable success in many situations over the last thirty or forty years.[116] Again, it has to be said that there are other theories of human behavior that would explain individual actions and that would be useful for practitioners who would presume to help others. However, because we need to get on with our work, we will not attempt here to discuss the host of theories, but rather will try to assess the uses of Freudian theory in social work practice in the modern urban era. It has often been said that the trouble with social casework is that it is "too Freudian," and it is hard to know what that means. If one uses a theoretical base for understanding behavior, be it

---

[116] Hamilton, Gordon, "A Theory of Personality: Freud's Contribution to Social Work," *Ego Psychology and Dynamic Casework,* Howard J. Parad, ed., Family Service Association of America, New York, 1958, pp. 11–37.

Rankian, Watsonian or Skinnerian, it is hardly possible to be "too" anything, because it is essential to know as much as possible about the content of the theoretical formulation being used. Perhaps the "too Freudian" accusation derives from the fact that, in truth, early social caseworkers stayed too close to the Freudian theoretical model of *treatment,* rather than to Freudian explanations of human behavior. The issue about Freudian theory and psychoanalytic treatment is very complicated, because the theory has been simultaneously defined, further refined, and practiced. Therefore, it has been exceedingly difficult to separate knowledge from application. In other words, as social casework theoreticians and practitioners sought to learn about Freudian theory, they had to study from psychoanalysts, who were practicing within their discipline and thereby discovering theoretical constructs. It is our view that the fusion between evolving psychoanalytic theory and practice had its adverse effect upon social casework practice because the line between the two was not drawn sharply enough. There are many unfortunate illustrations of this sad occurrence. For example, in schools of social work where practicing psychoanalysts have taught courses in human growth and behavior, they have demonstrated aspects of theory through illustrations of their own practice, and a generation of social workers has confused the theory with the practice. Another example can be found in the caseworker's predilection to know all, once having understood the concept of the unconscious. This route has led to therapeutic disasters, in that the unconscious has often represented the "all," and in the early days practitioners did attempt to bypass necessary ego defenses and search beyond them for root causes of behavior and for reorganization of unconscious ideation. A further example can be found in the current day when practitioners seek that one-to-one confrontation between worker and client, as if this were the preferred and only method of resolving human problems. Out of this preoccupation with the professional's expert knowledge of psychic processes and the object-client who appeared always in transference terms has evolved the appearance of a practice in social work that indeed looks as if it were a modified form of psychoanalytic practice requiring a maximum of social distance between worker and client.

Freudian theory of personality has undergone many changes as people like Erikson,[117] Hartmann,[118] and Menninger[119] have contributed to the expanding knowledge of ego psychology. It is this development that has provided for external expression of internal psychic processes and has, therefore, enhanced the possibility of a conceptual connection between the person and his environment. It has facilitated the entrance of nonpsychoanalytic practitioners, like social workers, into the arena of personality, for with the rediscovery of ego-functioning, it has become possible to address behavior without the use of psychoanalytic probing techniques into the hidden parts of personality.[120] As we shall see in Chapters 6 and 7, this possibility has significant implications for extensive social work intervention and differential uses of manpower.

An approach to viewing the personality as functioning along a broad range of balance to imbalance, has contributed to the current idea that treatment might relevantly be called *help* and not necessarily *therapy,* and that the signs of dysfunction are more appropriately diagnosed or assessed through viewing the individual in his own terms of reference, in his own life style, and not according to diagnostic labels; the clinic has moved outdoors. The person as a self-balancing system interacts reciprocally with the situational systems that are salient for him. Ideally society should provide through its established institutions the necessary supports and services that would reinforce the individual's capacity to cope with his life and functioning in that society.

---

[117] Erikson, *Op. cit.*

[118] Hartmann, Heinz, *Ego Psychology and the Problem of Adaptation,* Journal of the American Psychoanalytic Association, Monograph Series One, International Universities Press, New York, 1958.

[119] Menninger, *Op. cit.*

[120] Stamm, Isabel L., "Ego Psychology in the Emerging Theoretical Base of Casework," *Issues in American Social Work,* Alfred J. Kahn, ed., Columbia University Press, New York, 1959, pp. 80–109.

The person-in-situation configuration always has been the unit of attention in social casework, but the problem is that there is no total explanation of the entire concept. To the extent that personality theory presents a coherent whole, there has been a natural tendency to explain the two sides of the hyphen through the use of psychological knowledge. In order to understand the social situation, which, of course, has no base in personality theory, one has to draw upon fragmented theories in social science, like theories of social role, social class, cultures, groups, communities, family structures, reference groups, and social problems. Systems theory has provided the framework for reconceptualizing all knowledges in their reciprocal terms. As Devereaux wrote:

> The real objective is not to determine whether the phe-
> nomenon is ultimately a psychological or a socio-cultural
> one, but to analyze the dovetailing, interplay, and rein-
> forcement of all factors.[121]

As personality and social theories are measured by different yardsticks and are articulated in different languages on different levels of abstraction, we are still far from the state of unifying all knowledge of the person-in-situation under one theoretical awning.

Assuming that people seek in their own cultures and reference groups for modes of personal expression, it then becomes incumbent upon us to have specific knowledge of those socio-cultural forces. Further assuming that people function in accordance with particular, socially defined roles, the concept of social role becomes an essential part of the practitioner's knowledge repertoire. Finally, assuming that people intersect at all times with organizations that are the hallmark of urban society, knowledge of organizational theory and the way bureaucracy functions would need to share intellectual space with knowledge of the person. Thus according to Herman Stein's suggestion, social science at large provides for *substantive* knowledge about the nature

---

[121] Devereaux, George, "Two Types of Modal Personality Models," *Personality and Social Systems, Op. cit.,* p. 25.

of a particular society, ethnic group or a social class sub-culture, facts about the social structure of specific communities, the significance of distributions of various kinds of social data, and about specific behaviors under specific conditions. Social science also contributes *theoretical concepts* about the relationship between culture and personality, implications of bureaucratic cultures, and theories of social role, reference groups, family structures.[122]

We have said that all people live in a social context—albeit in individual ways—in their own specific life styles. Knowledge of the elements that comprise the individual's social situation may not be found all in the same place, and it may not be as immediately applicable as knowledge of personality, but as people are organismically related to their social milieu, there can be no conceptualization of feedback without the relevant knowledge of that milieu. It is as if only one child were on a seesaw: while the board is over to one side, it is impossible to assess the balance of the total mechanism. Thus, we see that the broadened parameters of the "case" create an intellectual challenge to the social work practitioner. The psychosocial situation that must be assessed in order to know what to do to help requires a systemic, organizing framework so as to make practice a possibility. Only in academic study can knowledge be an end in itself; the knowledge to which we have referred has its specific and particular uses for each individual client.

AIMS OF DIAGNOSIS

A result of reconceptualizing the unit of attention in the diagnostic process is that the purposes of diagnosis change. Schwartz and Schwartz have observed:

> From looking upon the process exclusively as a clinical activity, directed at a disease entity, and undertaken within the boundaries of the conventionally defined therapist-

---

[122] Stein, Herman D., "Social Science in Social Work Practice and Education," *Ego Psychology and Dynamic Casework, Op. cit.,* pp. 227–228.

patient relationship, the change is to seeing it, in addition, as a sociopsychological process that attempts to deal with problems in living that are not necessarily serious or well-defined emotional disorders.[123]

The implications to be drawn from this "reorientation" are vast, because old favored notions about the professional relationship, therapeutic techniques, causation, and cure inevitably must be modified. When the individual's own psychologically and culturally determined life-style becomes the unit of attention, the aim of practice would be to right the impaired balance; the issue would not be a problem to be solved, but rather a previous balance to be restored, or an improved balance to be established. "The therapeutic model has led to a search for primacy of problems underlying the presenting request or even unrelated to it."[124] The assumption of norms of behavior has heretofore governed the helping process, and has encouraged practitioners to seek the deepest causation for variance from the norm and ultimately to find a way to "cure" the perceived "illness" or problem. According to Schwartz and Schwartz, there has to be a distinction between treatment as a clinical procedure, and help that would follow the life process.

Returning to our conception of the case as a system of interacting and reciprocal forces, a practitioner might address any or all of the significant elements that are dysfunctional for the individual client and would seek in that field of influence, the adjustment of those factors that are proving disruptive. Where the aim of this diagnostic search is to be establishing a state of balance, then primary attention would have to be given to the nature of the present imbalance, the precipitating stress, the individual coping mechanisms to be enhanced, and the forces in the environment that can be mobilized to reinforce the individual's urge toward a self-righting balance in his specific situation. The

---

[123] Schwartz, Morris S. and Schwartz, Charlotte G., *Social Approaches to Mental Patient Care*, Columbia University Press, New York, 1964, p. 85.

[124] Germaine, *Op. cit.*

field of study, as we have mentioned, would comprise the individual and all of those people and institutions that affect and are affected by him, including the social worker himself and the service organization. This diagnostic field or unit of attention directs the practitioner to an immediacy of task definition and certainly expands both the parameters of the case and the nature of the job to be done.

The diagnostic process remains a useful tool for assessment of the case; it is the *case* that has extended its boundaries. The chief purpose of diagnosis still is to know what is relevant to do; it is the range of the intervention possibilities that has become enlarged. As the modern social work practitioner confronts the urban scene, with which he himself is systemically related, he will view the individual client as pivotal in a transactional field. Through "transactional sectioning" the practitioner will be able to select tasks of intervention, because in each salient "section" there will be a cross-section of the whole. This is not the same as partializing, where only a piece of the person's situation is addressed, because in systemic thinking, the person-in-situation is an organismic whole where all parts reverberate in each other.

The social work practitioner will need to be expert in his comprehension of the nature of human beings living in a complex urban environment, and his particular expertise will be found in his knowledge of how the person and the situation reinforce each other or, more likely, fail to do so. In our view of the unit of attention being the individual in his life style we have left behind the concept of clinically defined disease, and we might even have put aside the requirement of becoming a client in order to be helped by a social worker. Bringing together what we have observed earlier about the nature of the urban condition, the rising influence of public social institutions, and the broader conceptions of the individualizing process, we can now turn to discussion of the modes of social work practice intervention that could be reflective of all of these changing elements.

6

intervention through social work practice

> ... good professional social work is tested not
> by its difference but by its likeness to living
> well, living as a social being, and ... it gets
> its professional stamp from being practiced by
> people who make a special study and discipline
> of how to live.
>
> ——Bertha C. Reynolds

[125] Reynolds, Bertha Capen, *Social Work and Social Living,* Citadel
Press, New York, 1951, p. vi.

IT SHOULD BE EVIDENT, that traditional concepts about casework treatment need to be expanded so as to suit the expanded boundaries of the case. Yet, there is nothing more wrong with the term treatment than there is with the term diagnosis; it is only its connotations that are troublesome. It is not always desirable to create new terminology when one really wants only to redesign the meanings of the old, but to the extent that treatment (like diagnosis) represents a medical, disease-cure model, its use might obscure the necessity to view practice more broadly. For this reason, it might be more helpful to call the actions of the social work practitioner intervention.

THE ROLE OF PROFESSIONAL EXPERTISE

We noted in earlier chapters that new strains are running through the urban society having to do with racial conflict and the push toward community participation. It has become increasingly difficult in these days of heightened awareness of individual rights to self-determination to assert professional expertise in most practice roles. We have seen university presidents and faculties challenged by their students, school boards and teachers confronted by community parent groups, and mental health boards taken over by community forces. How much more influential would community groups be upon social work practice, in light of the fact that the work of social work appears to resemble so closely the daily common sense actions of people in their informal and official relationships with others. The concept of *intervention* into maladaptive systems provides for potential community participation without doing damage to the helpful purposes of expertise; the concept of *treatment* connotes a greater social distance between therapist and client, as if the role of expert could stand between service and the community. In moving away from the notion of disease, therapy, and cure toward the idea of health, natural life style, and righting the imbalance between individuals in their social milieu, an entirely different stance is available to the social work practitioner. It then becomes possible to imagine more interventive alternatives, greater use of differential manpower skills, greater direct attention to environmental variables that are within the diagnostic perimeters of the case, and an improved state of feedback about the terms of service, from the community to the professional practitioner.

The role of professional expertise is not only being held in question by students, blacks, and the poor people of the world, but as a quality of practice itself, from a professional point of view, it might need some qualification. We can draw a parallel between social work practice and an interesting observation made by Edmund Bacon in writing about urban planning.[126] He comments about the linear notion of a sequential progression in current thinking. By this he means that formulating goals through the well-known scientific process of getting the facts, analyzing them, and selecting a plan for implementation has little relationship to the total process occurring in urban life as we know it. He describes the essential feedback injected into the "tumult of democratic dispute in an ever recurring interaction." Assuming that social workers recognize the necessity to "democratize" practice, i.e., not only to bring services into the life of the community but also to have them become integral to the life style, demands, and needs of the community people, this circular vs. linear direction of expertise may be a very helpful concept. It means that every time a professional expert enters into community processes, which he must do if he is to approach his case as a transactional system, he will experience feedback. To the extent that he takes cognizance of the reverberations, he will bring his interventive processes as close as possible to the values existing in the community.

This process can be illustrated by imagining a case where a social worker through her contact with a client intends to help a community get a day-care center, working

---

[126] Bacon, Edmund, "Urban Process," *The Conscience of the City, Op. cit.*

on the assumption that a group of mothers who are on Aid to Dependent Children (ADC) want to go to work and need a place to leave their children. The facts of the situation may have indicated this "treatment plan" at least until other facts became known. Through the individualizing process, the worker would know what the mothers wanted, but until some of the organized groups in the community raised the issue of other alternatives, like increased ADC allowances or some other form of neighborhood care and support of the mothers and children, the mothers had been unaware of how they might be in control of different plans. Thus, the original plan becomes modified by the currents set loose in the community, possibly as a result of the entrance of the social worker into the situation. Bacon, in his discussion of urban planning, suggests that "In the process, the idea formulator himself has been tempered by the heat of his confrontation with his peers, and he himself, perhaps unwittingly, has become a more sensitive instrument more closely attuned to community values."[127] As worker and client are reciprocally influenced by each other, the hierarchy of status dissolves, and neither is "captive of the other." Thus the social work practitioner, expert in his knowledge of the meanings of the case, becomes part of a cyclical process of action. Reverberating feedback, from worker to client and back again, is the valve that protects the openness of systems, and this process somehow seems consonant with the revolutionary times in which we live.

Apart from the pressures of community people and constituent groups who are demanding their say, and apart from the pragmatic advantages of true reciprocity between practitioner and client, there are some other qualifying reasons for viewing expertise with restraint. Professional social work addresses people in their social situations without the aegis or tools to affect basic causes. Thus, although it may be evident that slum housing is a major cause of unhappiness and dysfunction in a case, the resolution of

---

[127] *Ibid.*, p. 1169.

the housing scandal in American cities does not rest with the social worker but probably rather with the politician. Although addictions are becoming a major social and health problem in this country, the multiplicity of factors that contribute to the problem have not been identified, and social workers, like doctors, are literally working in the dark without that basic knowledge. The urban crisis is so complex a phenomenon, it is quite doubtful that any single professional who dares to work with it directly will be capable of comprehending it. There are too many interweaving threads, and the problems are so ill-defined, while being at the same time so all pervasive, that it would be quite impossible to become expert in knowing it all.

We do not intend in this chapter to discuss techniques of intervention or treatment, for emphasis on techniques, as Merton says, tends to have "purposes revolve around what is useful rather than what is good," and we want to be free to explore the philosophy of practice, leaving practice skills to follow once the aims of practice are thoroughly aired. Merton further writes:

> Technique smothers the ideas that put its rule in question and filters out for public discussion only those ideas that are in substantial accord with the values created by a technical civilization.[128]

So as to keep our system of ideas as open as possible, we will hold out the hope that form will follow function, and that technique is not the largest of our worries.

REFLECTIONS ON PAST AIMS
OF CASEWORK PRACTICE

So as not to leave the impression with the reader that a new designation of interventive tasks in the individual's transactions with his environment means that social work intervention or treatment uses only new con-

---

[128] Merton, Robert K., Introduction to *The Technological Society,* Jacques Eilul, Vintage Books, New York, 1967, p. vii.

cepts, it would be well here to review some very fine definitions of practice in social casework. They will indicate that as far as intention was concerned, theorists in social work carved out a path which we are now following with a certain degree of inevitability.

Mary Richmond said in 1924:

> The specialized skill of the social caseworker will be found to be, in its essentials, just as applicable to the rest of the world as to those who could thus be labelled . . . (as separate groups of defined clients).[129]

Bertha Reynolds said in 1934, when she envisioned the availability of social casework at "the crossroads of life where ordinary traffic passes by" that:

> . . . no casework can succeed in isolating a person's attitudes and treating them apart from the conditions of his life in which they find expression.[130]

Fern Lowry said in 1938,

> Casework is nothing more or less than a method of helping individuals to meet such needs as are derived from the impoverishment of the environment or the limitations of individual capacity.[131]

Gordon Hamilton said in 1952,

> Casework reflects a trend in complex modern society to offer help with the personal aspects of ordinary living . . .[132]

Thus we see that some of the major theoreticians in social casework had some of the same aims we are verging

---

[129] Richmond, Mary E., *What Is Social Casework?*, Russell Sage, New York, 1922, p. 97.

[130] Reynolds, Bertha C., "Between Client and Community," *Smith College Studies*, 1934, pp. 37–38.

[131] Lowry, Fern, "Current Concepts in Social Casework Practice," *The Social Service Review*, Vol. XII, No. 3, Sept. 1938, pp. 365–373.

[132] Hamilton, *Op. cit., Theory and Practice of Social Casework*, p. 24.

on today, despite the fact that the "common human needs" theme along the "crossroads of life" became somewhat obscured by the preoccupations with clients who could be identified primarily in clinical terms. That trend assuredly led social caseworkers away from the citizenry at large who would never find their way to a clinic. We discussed in previous chapters that which is different in our society and in our knowledge that today would place the earlier reflections upon the aims of casework practice in quite a different framework. The fundamental purposes may remain the same, but the kind of practice and the what and how of practice naturally has had to change in response to changing times. It is this change that we are addressing in this book, this broadening of concepts about the case and what to do about it; we have just observed that the process was adequately described through the last fifty years and still has applicability once it is utilized in modern terms.

LEVELS OF INTERVENTION

Increasingly, material has appeared in recent years on preventive levels of social work intervention,[133] and even though it has been impossible to succeed in defining a preventive *practice* (as opposed to a philosophy of prevention), the struggle to find useful concepts about primary prevention have been salutary. The interest in prevention has pushed the social work effort back along the continuum of problems, so that it has begun to seek out causes before they become problems and has begun to find a new identity in being associated with health over disease. Rapoport has made a singular and quite courageous contri-

---

[133] Examples may be found in:

Council on Social Work Education, *Concepts of Prevention and Control: Their Use in the Social Work Curriculum*, C.S.W.E., 1961.

Council on Social Work Education, *Public Health Concepts in Social Work Education*, C.S.W.E., 1962.

Geismar, Ludwig L., *Preventive Intervention in Social Work*. Scarecrow Press, Metuchen, N.J., 1969.

bution to the discussions of prevention[134] by stating that the public health model of primary prevention cannot be adapted to social work practice because the causes of the problems that social work addresses have multiple roots in society, and social workers are not empowered to attack these in the way the public health doctor may fluoridate the water to prevent tooth decay or innoculate a population to prevent the onset of smallpox. Rapoport suggests that the borrowing of the concept of primary prevention is indiscriminate and overgeneralizing.

> It is more useful, therefore, to understand the interrelated parts of a complex system and to plan strategy which could interrupt at any one of several points, factors contributing to the development of pathology.[135]

Let us begin then with the assumption that early prevention methods theoretically are more effective than later rehabilitation efforts and that a responsible profession should seek all ways possible to keep problems from occurring, even though it may be most proficient at the time of the eruption of the problem. This statement warrants some clarification.

Analogously, in the medical profession there is a broad range of specializations along the health to disease continuum from public health doctor to neurosurgeon, for example. The surgeon is best qualified to operate and undoubtedly would hold a high priority for knowledge of brain pathology and technical surgical skills, for that is his craft. He will belong to associations that contribute to his work; he will confine his technical reading to his area; he will associate professionally with those doctors who share his interest, and above all he will undoubtedly view individual patients through the perceptions of a brain surgeon. In social work practice, with less justification, this professional preoccupation with one's specialty occurs as well.

---

[134] Rapoport, Lydia, "The Concept of Prevention in Social Work," *Social Work*, Jan. 1961.

[135] *Ibid.*, p. 9.

When a social caseworker is proficient in marital counseling, he tends to wait for the family to have a marital problem, so that he can practice his trade, as it were. Although it is true that family agencies are embarked on family life education programs in an effort to move into the preventive sphere, the clinical practitioner may still perceive families in the context only of marital problems. In child welfare, where clinical practice most often takes the form of child placement, intake usually means bringing into the placement process those children who are assumed to be without hope of continuing in life with their own families. It is not typical of modern child welfare practice that an established placement agency would seek preventive methods by moving their interventive process back a few years toward a problem-free era in the family's life. In public welfare the family in need must be impoverished in order to become a client, whereas earlier job training or day-care facilities might have prevented that abused status from ever occurring. In psychiatric and medical social work practice the individual must become a patient of the clinic or the hospital before he is paid attention to, even though the indicators of his physical or mental breakdown might have been in evidence earlier in the health-to-breakdown continuum.

In recent years social agencies have attended more to preventive measures through involvement in day care programs, homemaker services, job training, community mental health programs, outreach centers, etc., but it is interesting that it has been so difficult to define these measures in practice terms. In other words, when practice remains confined to clinical subjects and problem-laden entities, the tendency is to await their development, for that is where it must appear that the "real" work of practice occurs. Somehow the literature and practice seem to suggest that anything that occurs in the prediagnostic and prebreakdown sphere is policy or program, or that it belongs in the sphere of community organization. How does a neurological surgeon wield his scalpel through a fluoridating system, and how does a psychiatric social worker sharpen his verbal techniques through helping a welfare rights group to get organized? This seems to be the trouble social work practice is in; the technical specialists perceive the total organism perhaps, but the "problem to be worked" has become the paramount condition. It is our thesis that the narrowness in the field of attention that characterizes all specialists is due not only to professionalism and all of its ills but also to the fact that social work practice has not yet found a way to conceptualize prevention or early intervention, and thus it holds no real gratification for the serious practitioner who rightfully seeks a theoretical rationale for his work with individuals.

There have been many recent attempts in social work and in social psychiatry to invent new models of practice that would accommodate to the need to move into the preventive sphere. As we build our case here, we see that the aims of social work practice in order to be relevant to the present urban condition ought to be increasingly addressed to the citizenry at large and decreasingly to a clinically identifiable client group, to the natural life style of people, rather than to the "direct causal relationship between specific professional actions and change in the client's life."[136] This aim of practice will involve a major readjustment on the part of professional social workers, because it will make necessary some fundamental changes in the style of practice and in the self-image of the professional.

The transfer in aim from treatment to help, from disease to health, from cure to adaptation and greater comfort, and from client to citizen, will create some professional dilemmas in the present generation of social work practitioners. But it is the lot of the socially responsible professional to accommodate to the present scene and respond to the needs that are paramount and requisite. In other words, when there is a conflict in the streets between a

[136] Studt, Eliot, "Social Work Theory and Implications for the Practice of Methods," *The Council on Social Work Education Reporter*, June 1968.

community group and a professional group of teachers or social workers, is the higher value the "right of the professionals" to express their craft, or is it rather the obligation of the professional to listen to the demands of the citizenry and to try to meet their needs? That is the whole rationale of professions after all, but we know that professionalism becomes a force in its own right, indicating a functional autonomy or secondary rationale that superimposes itself on the first reason for professional action.

Two models of practice that seem to qualify as reflective of the modern scene are *crisis intervention* and Eliot Studt's presentation of *strategy and task*. We shall explore these two approaches in some detail, but as we have said, there is only validity to a model of practice when it is couched in a meaningful framework. Therefore we shall recapitulate and attempt to tie together some of the philosophical threads we have been weaving through this book in an effort to evaluate the usefulness of either or both of these illustrative models of practice.

We have described a view of the urban scene of today, where all citizens seem to have to rely on social institutions external to them and their family for the physical-socio-economic requisites of life. Thus, when all citizens have need of something, and for the moment we need not specify that something, it becomes inappropriate to define them as clients, which term implies a degree of dependency upon another for service, advice, or advocacy. It is almost as if one were to say that a battalion of soldiers are all neurotic because they are fearful of battle and are in need of treatment, or that a crowd of people on the street who have waited for an hour for a bus are all neurotically hostile toward the transportation system and in need of help. We have said that urban life creates situational disorders just by virtue of its existence, and that its effects upon the citizenry are more or less undiscriminating. Even while the poor populations or neighborhoods are clientele with strains in urban life, it would be difficult to assert that they have clinically defined problems when poverty and the city are themselves the problem. Thus in a psycho-situational diagnosis the individual's problem may be the city, which is not quite subject to the ministrations of the social work practitioner, when it is hardly "treatable" by political organizations and mayors.

We are not overlooking the fact of differences in the capacities of individuals to cope with strains in urban living, for as a result of individualizing, one can determine the particular balance, forces, and interactions that make every person-situation different from every other. To individualize is not to address a client in dysfunctional terms. We are in the midst of an age of revolution where rights and participation are the watchwords and where professional experts who have the authority of knowledge, social distance, and the control of their offices are suspect. The term assigned to the person who is helped by the social work practitioner is not important here; rather, as in our discussion of diagnosis and treatment, it is more important to consider the difference in role and the meaning of the term. When individuals are perceived as being in a dysfunctional or imbalanced state in their environment, and not, therefore, considered to be diseased, they can be called client or claimant or patient or customer or consumer or student or constituent or citizen. It is not the appellation that we hold in question, but rather the meaning it holds for practice.

AVAILABILITY OF SOCIAL WORKERS
AT THE "CROSSROADS"

If we can move ahead on the assumption that urban living has made all citizens potential "clients," and so all clients potential nonclinically defined consumers of social work services, some strategies for social work practice flow inevitably from these assumptions. The matter of location is a crucial one, for availability at "the crossroads of life" is essential if the practitioner is to meet the citizen. The clinic, therefore, must move outdoors;

the old notion of the "Little Red School House and Little White Clinic"[137] must be reevaluated and the definition of problem must be broadened to some nonprejudicial notion like imbalance, and the social distance of the social work practitioner must be reduced. Furthermore, we know where the stress points are in the urban scene, and it is at those places where practitioners will have to be prevalent in order to provide the greatest degree of preventive intervention.

Earlier, in Chapter 4, we presented a developmental chart that suggested that social work practice could be conceptualized as being influential along a developmental scheme of human life. These are indeed intersections at developmental and transitional crisis points in the lives of all individuals. Let us try here to operationalize that developmental chart depicting the individual and his transitional interactions with social institutions; let us try to imagine where social work practice will stand in these interactional location points.

As a location "in time," we might start with birth, surely the first of the developmental crises for the infant, and one of a series for the parents and relatives. In keeping with our commitment to stay with prevention as much as possible, let us envisage a social work program in a prenatal clinic. In the next chapter we will discuss in detail the role of nonprofessional manpower, for we must be certain not to confuse the presence of social work practice with insistence upon the professional at all points. In a prenatal clinic, there will be the usual range of concern on the part of the pregnant mothers, going from complete acceptance of the fact of the coming baby and sufficient resources to cope with the new member of the family, to severe anxiety on the part of an unwed mother who may be immobilized by the forthcoming responsibility. Pregnancy always brings with it a certain degree of normal anxiety. In the urban situation where extended family life is so difficult to pursue, the pregnant mother might not have the support of her own

[137] White, Mary Alice, "Little Red Schoolhouse and Little White Clinic," *Teacher's College Record*, Dec. 1965.

mother's presence, and if she is poor, she has a chance of not having the baby's father at home. Her problem will be intertwined with her condition, and to some extent she might have all the reassurance she needs from the doctor who is attending to her pregnant condition. Yet the matter of planning for the baby, for income while the mother is not working, for care of the older children at home, for future planning about childbirth, for the housing squeeze she might be anticipating, and for the idiosyncratic factors that are marks of her individual case will be in evidence. Moreover, the natural tensions, occurring between the mother and the soon-to-be displaced father and the children at home, may be of some burden to the pregnant mother. To describe the lot of the pregnant mother waiting in the prenatal clinic is to describe the natural life situation of all pregnant mothers, citizen and not "client" mothers in this situation.

Help may range from a kind word, a supportive arm, a telephone call to the welfare department or intervention with the medical personnel, to a long talk to air the tensions the mother is feeling, to a longer talk where she might use reflective processes to wonder about herself and her patterns of behavior. The point is that the very presence of the individualizing practitioner, who might in this case at first be a nonprofessional social worker, in itself might serve to prevent the ultimate rejection of the new baby, or the slow torture of marital conflict that could develop. Furthermore, as we will discuss when we analyze the contribution of crisis intervention theory, the developmental crisis of pregnancy might in some instances be the very moment when the mother is most accessible to help for a long-standing psycho-social problem that has been bothering her and interfering with her happiness. The point is that the location on the scene of the natural life event will in itself make help available and more possible. The reader will note that we have not asked of the mother that she go downtown for an appointment, that she sign up, or be highly motivated for treatment, or that she define herself into a typical client role. Shlakman notes that:

> Social welfare services have either been tangential to the population-at-risk, or deterrent in philosophy and practice.[138]

We might illustrate any of the intersectional points of relationship between the person and the social institution, such as the nursery school when the child attends for the first time, and the mother feels she cannot leave him. Or we might follow the child's career through school and its entrances and graduation times, or the parents' employment career, or the daily life processes in which everyone partakes. At each point there may be no *problem*, or there may be; at each point there is the necessity to negotiate the city and the bureaucratic institutions that have come to characterize it.

SOME RESTRAINTS ON INTERVENTION

In attempting to locate individualizing services "in space" or at those places where people intersect in the normal course of their lives, we are of course entering the institutional or developmental sphere of social welfare, in contradistinction to the more familiar residual sphere. Prior to exploring a legitimate role for social work practice in locations where "preproblem" circumstances occur, it is important to address some difficult questions. Let us suppose that adequate social insurance programs were to supplant the present public assistance method of providing income maintenance. People would then receive income on the basis of their status in a predefined group that is judged by the Congress to be vulnerable to average expectable and

---

[138] Shlakman, Vera, "Mothers-at-Risk: Social Policy and Provision, Issues and Opportunities," *Mothers-at-Risk*, Florence Hazelkorn, ed., Adelphi University School of Social Work, Garden City, N.Y., 1966, p. 67.

natural risks of life. With the termination of the means test and the eligibility study, where social workers traditionally have determined individual need on a case-by-case basis, and the coming of the universally agreed upon right of all citizens to an adequate income, we need to ask *what role social work practice would have in such an objective income maintenance scheme.* Social insurance means that need is defined in terms of universal risks that are applicable to the total population and not in terms of personal failure or individual problem. Thus, if we are to contemplate the use of social work practice in a social insurance system, we would surely need to re-examine the definitions of practice which presently relate individualizing services to people with defined problems, or we would be guilty of turning the clock back and imposing a residual coloration on an institutional program. If we personalize an appropriately impersonal program, will this attention to the individual damage the concept of universality and objectivity? This is a most difficult problem, for a modern social worker would not want to confuse the insurance concept by defining need on a case to case basis when government has advanced to the point of defining need through legislation and statute. The problem can be solved by maintaining a separation between the income maintenance program and the social work service and by treating the social insurance office as if it were a "community." Although the social worker has no role in an objective income maintenance program, the social security office is in fact, an ideal location for case-findings in a developmental scheme of social work.

The typical social security office presents an atmosphere that is markedly different from that of the urban public assistance office. The latter is often in a run-down condition; staff is overwhelmed by pressures; clients struggle through the bureaucratic obstacles in order to get their basic needs met; the total morale in the system suffers from cynicism, discrimination against the poor and against the people who work with them; and the atmosphere is permeated with an attitude of scapegoatism. On the other hand, the social security office, because it is a federal agency, is an insurance instead of an assistance program, and is financially and attitudinally further removed from the local citizen taxpayer, it does not suffer from the same characteristics as the public assistance agency. The office is usually pleasant, the furniture modern, the equipment up-to-date, and the personnel well-trained to their well-defined tasks of connecting the claimant with his rightful income. Staff training is mostly directed toward developing attitudes of acceptance and responsiveness,[139] because the staff's primary tasks are not substantive. They do not decide who is eligible; they do not have the authority to rule claimants in or out of the social insurance system. Rather, laws, policies, and ultimately machines govern those decisions. Thus in the British spirit, a worker in social insurance is primarily a civil servant carrying out the nation's policies that are determined elsewhere. The dissatisfied claimant who has exhausted his benefits must take his concern to the politician, and the office itself becomes merely a corridor through which is exchanged rights and income. It is obvious that quite a different purpose is served in social security and public assistance offices, and as form follows function, there is no individualizing service performed in the social security office. This is why one must be alert to the question about the role of social work practice in a structure that has, up to now, wisely kept itself removed from the stigma of traditional, residual social work practice.

Returning in our discussion to the role of social work practice in a developmental scheme of social welfare, the social insurance office is a most desirable location for individualized services because it is used by increasing numbers of citizens who typically have not yet articulated problems sufficiently to gain them entrance into the range of possible client systems that might be connected with residual social work agencies. What a fine location in which

---

[139] de Schweinitz, Karl and Elizabeth, *Interviewing in Social Security,* U.S. Dept. of HEW, Washington, D.C., 1961.

we might explore the possibilities for early social work intervention.

Who, after all, goes to that office at the present time? According to law, every individual in the Social Security system who is to receive Medicare, the man who has arrived at retirement age, the woman whose husband has just died, the young children in a family whose father has been killed in an industrial accident, and if social insurance programs proliferate as we expect they will, there will be more statuses of people there. For example, family allowances will mean that citizens will become attached to their local social insurance offices as much and as often as they become connected with any other single institution in society. And they will not all be poor or disadvantaged in other ways, or sick or old or addicted or delinquent. They will be people who will represent the total range in society; they will represent all classes, ethnic groups, ages and degrees of social adaptation. They will be sick and they will be well, and most of them will be average in every regard, because by its definition social insurances define average status in the citizenry.

At the time of their contact with the social security office they presently are enduring some psychological and social crisis, as expressed in their need for economic rearrangements. At present, referrals to social agencies are usually made by receptionists, or claims clerks, but in such instances, people must make themselves "cases." They must articulate a problem, find the motivation to pursue a referral, and actually conceptualize their difficulty as a social work problem, thereby permitting themselves to enter a stigmatized client system. That is the way it is now.

The use of social work practitioners or their nonprofessional designates as individualizers of the social insurance system need not interfere with the objectivity of the program nor with the desires of some people to not have help. Availability is probably the key principle, for most people in the urban complex can use help in negotiating their lives, and most particularly do those people need help who are under the strain of crisis events in their lives. As the nature of help is usually characterized by the structure in which it is provided, help in this instance would undoubtedly range from listening to a recently widowed woman who needs to talk about her husband to actively arranging with her for a different way of living. The entire spectrum of life is represented in the social security office, and it would seem to be a most likely location to provide evidence of the government's concern with the individualizing of social systems, beginning with its own federal program. As long as the individualizing services are not admixed with the primary income maintenance program, nor with any other requirements except the claimant's need and desire for help, it can be demonstrated theoretically that the two levels of service can exist without contaminating each other's aims.

ORGANIZATIONAL BOUNDARIES

Heretofore, we have commented upon several kinds of boundaries in our presentation of social work practice in the urban scene. Recalling Chapter 1, we raised questions about existing methodological boundaries that presently separate social casework and group work and community organization. In Chapter 5 we proposed that "the case" had potential boundaries that could include the individual in his transactional field. The expansion of methodological and case boundaries quite naturally would lead to a similar expansion in the boundaries of settings in which practice takes place: when cases cannot really be understood or worked with in the more or less narrow policies of agencies in which they are found; when, in fact, cases actually reach out beyond agency boundaries, then the base of operations of practice would have to be redefined. This is not to say that practice is organizationally rootless, but rather that as cases transcend the functions of most single function or even multiple function social agencies, there needs to be a different way of conceptualizing the organizational boundaries which contain "the case" and the practitioner. Thus the settings of child welfare and family agencies, psychiatric and medical clinics, or hospitals may often be too narrow in concept for the stretch of the case. We have begun to suggest that there are other organizational forms that might be more capable of patterning themselves after the life style of individuals, for example, the well-baby center and the social security office. These two kinds of institutions represent typical modern urban life requirements for the average citizen. The pressing need from increased population and the proportionate lack of doctors have made the general hospital or the well-baby center the modern equivalent of the private doctor's office; the reliance in a technical urban society upon money income and the necessity to draw upon social insurance instead of reduced personal resources will enhance the popular use of the social security office. These "agencies" are increasingly becoming the outposts of normal family life; they are potentially part of the life style of all families; and they require limited articulation of "problem" in order to be used. As the families who would typically make use of such services, as provided by these and other similar institutional programs are theoretically in the nonclinical state of "preproblem," any attention paid to them by a social work practitioner would be on a level of early intervention. As we have said earlier, the *location* of the practitioner in the intersecting points where individuals and their significant situations meet ultimately will determine the relevance of practice in the modern urban scene. As the possible locations are as manifold as there are extra-family social institutions, it will be necessary to devise a scheme for looking at them.

As it is one of the major theses of this book that people in the modern urban society are in need of individualizing, one of the variables to be considered in classifying the organizational bases of social work practice must be the potential *numbers of people* that can be served. A second thesis is related to the matter of *early intervention*; thus another variable would be the degree to which the location of practice is close to or removed from the clinical definitions of problem. A third thesis of this book has to do with viewing the case in *systemic terms,* so a third variable to be considered will be the extent to which the organizational unit provides for assessment of and intervention in the case in systemic terms. So we will devise an organizing framework for practice that is an extension of the natural life style of cities and of people who live in them.

In the present organizational scheme of social work, we will develop our discussion, moving from the smallest unit out to the unit that provides for all of the above-mentioned criteria.

At the narrowest end of the scale, we should take note of social workers in *private practice,* who, while not actually representative of an organizational arrangement, nonetheless number at *least* 200[140] out of a 1965 estimate of 25,000 professional social workers in this country.[141] Analogous to the private practitioner in medicine and law, social workers in private practice must select a small number of client-patients who are able to pay, who suit predetermined criteria for help, who generally would be highly motivated and who are judged to be best able to use the expert help being offered. These characteristics would place the work of the private practitioner quite far inside of the clinical sphere, and due to limitations of the practitioner's time and resources, the client's field of transaction or the unit of attention would need to be quite narrowly defined.

On the second level, moving out from this smallest structural and, in fact, nonorganizational unit, will be the established voluntary social agency, compartmentalized into mental health clinics, family or child welfare functions and

---

[140] This is the number registered in the *North American Directory* of the Conference for the Advancement of Private Practice in Social Work, 1965. This would be the lowest estimate of all professional social workers in private practice.

[141] Baker, Mary, "Personnel in Social Work," *Encyclopedia of Social Work,* National Association of Social Workers, New York, 1965, p. 539.

occasionally combining these. As these are voluntary agency structures, they have some characteristics similar to the private practitioner except in some cases for the payment of fees. They may define their own intake policies, and select only those clients who will best use their defined services, and they may expand or contract their services in accord with agency program policy, availability of funds, and staff resources. Like the private practitioner, they cannot respond to the expression of need on any large scale, and they tend to stay inside of clinical boundaries so as to relate defined client groups to their defined programs. They differ markedly from private practitioners, however, when it comes to their potential capacity to intervene in the client's salient transactional field.

The third level of agency structure is the social service program in a voluntary mental or general hospital, where the social work practitioner usually must adapt to the primary function of the parent institution and deal to a greater or lesser degree with patients in the total small system of the hospital. This will bring the practitioner, while still in the clinic structure, in contact with patients that are defined more broadly than in social service functional terms. Even though hospitals may often define their services narrowly in terms of the need in the community, once defined, those eligible people become the medical responsibility of the hospital, and thus the responsibility of the social work practitioner. To the degree that clinical and preventive mental and physical care services move out of the walls of the hospital, which is occurring increasingly, the social work service will find itself out in the street as well, making it increasingly possible to include more people, on an earlier level of intervention, more in accord with the normal pursuit of their lives.

The fourth level of agency structure, still in the voluntary sphere, is the settlement house, which usually serves the total neighborhood surrounding it, or at least a portion of that neighborhood that by some status is eligible for the individual and group and community action services of the agency. Even though some settlement houses have gone the route of establishing clinical services within their agencies, therefore placing them in level two of our scheme, they generally define their services more broadly and theoretically as appropriate to membership organizations that may be more responsive to the natural life style of people in the community.

In the voluntary social service structure, then, we have the following picture:

Private practitioner → Child welfare and institutions / Family services / Mental health clinics → Hospitals / Settlement houses

Assuming the community to be the neighborhood or the client group defined according to statuses, kinds of symptoms expressed, behavior problems, or relationship problems, these agencies under voluntary auspices ordinarily address themselves to a number of people in the urban environment. With greater resources in staff and money they might even bring in more clientele, and, theoretically speaking, they might devise branch offices, or they might add more of the same kinds of agencies so as to cover the city. However, one or two restraints remain, among them the fact that no voluntary agency is accountable to the community at large. Even when it receives governmental subsidies, it is free to protect nonsubsidized programs and occasionally may not be subject to careful public control when the services they offer are desperately needed in the city. It is conceivable that additional black or Puerto Rican agencies, for example, might fill in the service gap, but it is doubtful that such agencies would be able to afford purely voluntary status or even that they would be capable of expanding their services sufficiently to meet the total community need in the city.

Looking now at public or governmental agencies, we might at times find them to be offering parallel services to those offered by voluntary agencies, but the crucial differences lie in their accountability to the public at large through legislative mandate and taxpayers' approval of program and budgets through the offices of elected officials. The public support and control of governmental agencies means that, as in law, all people are technically eligible through a defined status for the service provided by a particular agency. It is, of course, a serious peril to services when public agencies define the client status too narrowly, so that large numbers of citizens may not take advantage of the potential help available. But once defined, intake policies cannot rule out people by virtue of their treatability or their social affiliations through class, race, or religion. This factor brings the public agencies out into the community arena, perhaps still in the clinic in some instances, but at least in a position of responsibility for all of the people who may need that clinic. Thus we see public departments of social service or welfare that will combine child welfare, public assistance, homemaker services, etc. Each will have its defined intake policies, but they will be available to all of those people who have articulated their needs or who have been sent to the agency involuntarily. We may list social services in the public courts, schools, hospitals, clinics, and day care centers, all among a growing list of proliferating agencies in which social work practice takes place.

We have noted that in all of the agencies, both voluntary and public, social work help usually is offered on the basis of a defined need for counseling, group experiences, money, psychiatry, child placement, services for the aged, the sick, the disabled, etc. These various kinds of problem definitions, once having been made, make possible social work assistance in either kind of agency. The question we have, of course, is what is to be done about those vast numbers of people who (1) have not yet arrived at a clinically defined state of being, or (2) have no experience or capacity to articulate their need for clinical service, or (3) have a sense of resistance about going for help to an office or clinic which is not part of their natural style of living.

Thus, no matter how much we may expand clinical services, it is unlikely that the entire city would ever become "covered" with available services unless we were willing to assign clinical syndromes to every inhabitant of the city.

We have looked at agency functions and programs in relationship to their closeness to the larger community and their ability to serve large numbers of people, early in the process of psycho-social breakdown, in the total sphere of their transactions. There is yet another way to examine agency operations in light of criteria of accessibility and responsiveness to community need, and that is to view their *organizational structure*. All organizations, large and small, public or private, are bureaucratic. This is not a pejorative term necessarily, even though there are many effects of bureaucracy that are not salutary. By way of review for the reader, the characteristics of a bureaucracy are fully presented by Merton, Weber, *et al.*[142] Staff organizations based upon hierarchical status achieved through promotions, seniority, or advanced skills are an inevitable requisite of social agencies that utilize professional practitioners. The well-known paper work is also a hallmark of social work organizations because clientele and staff and administrative actions must be kept track of. This doesn't mean that professionals must always do that paper work. In all social work organizations there must be defined policies that will explain programs, but this does not mean that policies must be narrow or rigid. When agencies become bureaucratized, they begin to exist for their own ends, and this fact then leads to lack of real responsiveness to community need.

The war on poverty and the existence of public and private project funds have contributed to the design of a different kind of agency structure that was intended to

---

[142] Merton, Robert K., *et al.*, eds. *Reader in Bureaucracy,* Free Press of Glencoe, Ill., 1952.

Weber, Max, *The Theory of Social and Economic Organization,* trans. A. M. Hederson and Talcott Parsons, Oxford University Press, London, 1947.

carry the advantageous attributes of voluntary and governmental structures without their organizational restraints. They were devised to be close to the group of people being served, to provide for maximum participation of the clientele in the programs, and to be loose agencies not fettered to bureaucratic and hierarchical functions. The financial supports come from large foundations or from OEO or a combination of these. According to the scale we have introduced, this kind of agency structure would surely be placed out into the heart of the arena of people being served; springing out of community concern, they would be responsive to community need. It is still too early to evaluate this new kind of agency in any depth, although there are some current studies which raise questions about the actual successes of even these agencies.[143] It would seem that programs that are devised to cope mainly with problems of poverty and social disability may be doomed from the start because of their built-in scapegoatism (in line with Titmuss's thinking, Chapter 1). Moreover, the creation of new agencies does not necessarily mean the reduction of bureaucracy just because they are new, even when the problems to which they attend have been reconceptualized.

It might be considered here that there is no way to provide extraclinical or preclinical services to an urban population through any type of social agency, public, voluntary or project-type, simply because the purpose of the agency will have to be defined about a problem, whether it be poverty, marital conflict, child neglect, or aging. It seems to be an organizational fact that when an agency is developed to cope with a problem, even when the problem is broadly defined, it tends to view life in those terms, and thus begins the process of exclusion of people without those defined problems.

Let us look at another kind of structure that might meet the criteria we have established, of responsiveness and availability to community need, at the highways and by-

---

[143] See Chap. 1 for references to Marris, Rein, and Moynihan.

ways, wherever people go in the natural course of their lives. We are not saying here that clinical services are not functional for their purposes. Rather that in the course of conceptualizing the notion of preventive social work practice, it is essential to redraw the definitional boundaries of social work organizations in order to locate social workers where people are. Generally people are not at the doors of any clinic or agency until they have articulated a problem, or until someone else has noticed one; in order to reach them through early intervention, it would seem obvious that practice would have to be associated with "normal" everyday institutions with which people are involved in the course of their lives.

Developmental social work practice would occur wherever social institutions exist to serve people in specialized areas of their lives. In the main, these are health and educational institutions, employment offices, police and fire stations, housing, religious institutions, social security agencies, license bureaus, libraries, day-care centers, and social utilities of the kind described by A. J. Kahn. Furthermore, in the private or commercial sphere, we similarly ought to view labor unions and shopping centers as likely locations for the provision of individualizing services at the places where people go in their pursuit of their daily, complicated lives in the city of today. Let us be certain that we are not proposing that social work services be imposed upon people, but simply that they be available at times of stress. Also we are not saying that social work services would take the place of the primary service being offered in any of the institutions or locations just mentioned. Rather we are suggesting that bureaucratic structures break down in the area of individualizing when they become too large and too specialized in the function they are established to perform, and that as organizational services have come to replace family and other intimate supports, there is a need for such agencies to provide that intimate function of individualizing, relating, advocating, and helping people to connect appropriately with the service being offered.

In a school the teacher is supposed to teach; that is his primary function, and he must be given the time and opportunity to do that. When school social work services are placed in a clinical setting, sometimes outside the school building itself, the child's problems must be defined clinically, in order for a referral to be affected. Furthermore, the lack of presence of a social worker in the building makes it almost impossible for the teacher, the child, or the parent to make use of his services at the moment of stress. The model we propose might have a roaming social worker or team of professionals and nonprofessionals present in the school and part of the broad educational responsibility of the school system. Assuming that the work of the school is to educate children, this means that all children are known to the schools, and they are potentially the community to which the social worker attends; the school boundaries in the neighborhood thus become the social worker's catchment area. As the social institution, which is used by all families in the area, it would seem a likely place to pick up incipient family troubles that would range from lack of solvency to marriage conflicts to parent-child problems. The PTA, for example, would be a logical place for a social work service that would be addressed to some kind of specific social action, and the halls and the lunchroom would be ideal offices for the preventive social work practitioner.

In a hospital, there are many models of social work service, some that are built around medical clinical entities which follow the doctor's practice and some that are more general and exist somewhat outside or on the fringe of the medical practice and provide services in their own right. For example, a social work service might be connected with all of the specialized clinics in the hospital that are, after all, expressions of the expertise developed in several areas of medicine; they are not the way people are in general. People are not fractures or infectious diseases or skins, etc. Yet it has been administratively tidy to connect social workers with those clinics that focus on specialized medical problems, without reference to the integral social work service itself. Another model of medical social work practice is where the social work service might exist as a generalist organization, available for direct service to all patients and for consultation to all hospital staff when needed. As in the school we have envisioned, the social work practitioner might simply be present in a waiting room and be observant about incipient problems that might or might not be connected with the illness that brought the family to the hospital. As in the school where education is the purpose, the services of the hospital must be directed toward medicine, but people bring their total concerns with them, wherever they go. Thus, an available social worker with an individualizing function would be located in such a way as to pick up problems before they are articulated in advanced clinical terms.

We might generalize from schools and hospitals to all other social institutions and private commercial establishments, each having their own function and each needing that special individualizing service that could be made available by social work practitioners.

In examining the various kinds of organizational schemes that form the present and potential boundaries for social work practice, it appears that individualizing services need not be defined by the nature of the setting in which they occur. Yet a practitioner might select an area of specialization from the entire range of human activity, which is from health, disease, education, labor, delinquency, child neglect. Specialized knowledge about the area in which the practitioner chooses to work would be essential for him to become expert in the salient systems that would describe the case.

As we view the modern social work practitioner as a specialist in individualizing services at the crossroads of urban life, we then must seek appropriate methods of work. New models of practice are being developed that seem to have particular relevance to the framework we have been discussing. Modes of crisis intervention and definitions of strategy and task seem to hold very good potential, and we will discuss them as *illustrative* of approaches that would meet the requirements of social work practice in the urban scene. We have noted those requirements as being:

1. To serve as many people as quickly and parsimoniously as possible.

2. To view individuals in their natural life situation as part of their transactional field.

3. To provide for re-establishment of psycho-social balance rather than for "long-term" therapeutic efforts at "cure."

4. To intervene directly to strengthen individual coping mechanisms and to reinforce social supports.

CRISIS INTERVENTION THEORY

Crisis intervention is a most useful theory for a model of early interventive social work practice. It really makes necessary the accessibility and availability of the practitioner at all potential crisis points in the individual's life. It is important to the integrity of the theory of crisis intervention[144] that crisis as a human phenomenon not be defined too broadly, or it will lose its value as a psychosocial term of precision. As a discrete concept, it is not intended to be a diffuse umbrella for such happenings as an emergency, an acute onset of an illness, nor another word for being upset. A crisis, according to Rapoport[145] and others, is the reaction of a human being in a hazardous situation which makes for upset in a steady state; crisis treatment thus is directed toward the re-equilibrium of that upset state. In a crisis situation, it is theorized that one's natural or adaptive mechanisms are not working, and that, as the defenses are down, as it were, the individual's anxiety is heightened, and he is then available to help not only for the problem he faces immediately but also for older prob-

---

[144] Parad, Howard J., ed., *Crisis Intervention*, Family Service Association, New York, 1965.

[145] Rapoport, Lydia, "The State of Crisis: Some Theoretical Considerations," in *Crisis Intervention*, *Op. cit.*, pp. 22–31.

lems that are echoed in the present one. According to crisis theory, the event that triggers the crisis reaction may be viewed either as a threat or a challenge to the individual who must cope with it. There is either an adaptive or a maladaptive solution, and when help is given to support new adaptive mechanisms, these may be on a higher level of functioning than the previous ones. Therefore, it is theorized that the person will have improved adaptive mechanisms as a result of mastering the crisis.

The theory of crisis intervention has roots in significant developments in knowledge about human behavior. As is fully discussed in Menninger's *The Vital Balance*,[146] the core concept in human psychology is the equilibrating effect of the ego, the compensatory actions taken consciously and unconsciously by the ego to maintain a balance of forces and energy both within the person and between the person and his immediate environment. As attention is paid to ego functions and its adaptive, as well as defensive capacities, we are able to address the ego as an autonomous force. This means that cognitive understanding of a situation will lead toward its mastery, and that actual tasks given and mastered by the person will strengthen ego capacities. Assuming the theory of neutralized energy, people can change for consciously determined reasons in accordance with their mindful view of the alternative paths of action available to them and not only for libidinal gains that remain hidden and inaccessible through ordinary means. The emphasis given in crisis theory to recognition of the crisis as opposed to denial of it illustrates the wedding of the theory with the core concept of autonomous ego-functioning. Cognitive mastery of the crisis has tremendous implications for the role that modern social work practice may play in crisis situations, for "explanations" of what is happening to a person may well be a therapeutic task that need not be confined to a professional practitioner's repertoire. We shall have more to say in the next

---

[146] Menninger, *Op. cit.*, Chap. V., pp. 76–96.

chapter about manpower strategies in relation to crisis theory.

Crisis theory has roots in the contribution of Erik Erikson[147] in his work on maturational tasks and natural life crises, in the work of Erich Lindemann[148] and others, as well as in the epidemiological concepts of mental health. The delineation of the person's life work to master the natural crisis events of his age-specific situation has enhanced the development of crisis theory as an interventive social work practice method.

Public health concepts have also provided part of the bedrock for the development of crisis theory, in that the interest in prevention and epidemiology served to propel the Harvard School of Public Health to study natural life crises concerning the birth of premature children, hospitalization of mothers with TB, etc. The characteristics of crisis intervention theory that follows the public health model have to do with the immediacy of help at the onset of the crisis reaction, and the availability of service at those locations where crisis is most apt to occur. A further occurrence in recent years that has supported the development of crisis intervention theory that has made it seem syntonic with our age has been the recrudescence of existentialism and the emphasis on the primary importance of the present.

So we see that crisis intervention theory is rooted in a modern philosophy of life and an extension of Freudian theory particularly as it has been developed by ego theorists like Hartmann, Menninger, and Erikson. Its practice model is partly public health and the interest in early prevention of breakdown and partly community psychiatry and social casework with their recent attention to ego-functioning and coping capacities.

Now that we have a skeletal idea of the meaning of the theory of crisis, we can backtrack slightly, look at some definitions of crisis, and try to relate these to our thesis

---

[147] Erikson, *Op. cit.*

[148] Lindemann, Erich, "Symptomatology and Management of Acute Grief," in *Crisis Intervention, Op. cit.*, pp. 7–21.

about the role of social work practice in the by-ways of life. Taking Erikson first, there are maturational crises to which we have already alluded; the requirements at each stage of life of mastering those tasks that go with that stage, before it is possible on the maturational scale for people to graduate to the next level of maturity. Assuming the validity of this theory of maturation, would it not appear logical, in accordance with our chart in Chapter 4, for social work practice to locate itself at those points of convergence between the individual at all ages and those social institutions where he must exercise his mastery? The same may be said for role-transitional crises, where individuals move from one status to another and have difficult tasks of mastery. A typical example may be found in the first year of college, when young people so often find the adjustment from child to self-propelling independent young adult a great strain on their familiar coping mechanisms. Universities make provision for this through orientation programs, big brother and sister arrangements, house deans, and guidance counselors. The assumption that the role-transitional crisis is a natural one for the college-age person means that malfunctioning at this stage is not to be considered as pathological. Could we say less about the migration to the cities of the rural poor minority group, or the forced moving of neighborhoods to make way for urban redevelopment, or the strain upon families whose adolescent children find new outlets that are alien to the culture of their parents?

Another form of "natural life crisis" may be found in those that occur as a result of natural catastrophes like tornadoes, fires, ship sinkings, etc. In our society there are models for crisis help through the actions of the Coast Guard, the Red Cross or the Fire Department. It is accepted that not only must the physical aspect of the crisis be taken care of but also that the individuals who suffer the crisis must be cared for in particular ways. Social institutions have structured help when crisis strikes, and although the steps may not be outlined as precisely or theoretically as in crisis theory, the intention to ease people through the crises that are externally determined has been institutionalized throughout history.

The crisis situation that is most familiar to social work practitioners may be called, in crisis terms, the self-induced or pseudo-crisis, which is actually adaptive and is often the problem that develops from poor ego management due to intellectual or psychic causes. Here we refer to the range of interpersonal problems that have clinical manifestations —the sadomasochistic marital relationship that results in a series of "crisis events," the suicidal person, the neurotic child who is caught stealing, the disturbed mother who abuses her child, etc. Society has also arranged through clinics, courts, and social agencies to cope with self-induced crises, but only at those points where they can be defined clinically.

All types of crises have similar results in that they are all ego-disorganizing phenomena which means that tension is increased, functioning is impaired, and identity is threatened. The aim of crisis treatment is, wherever possible, to restore the person to the last best previous balance he was able to effect before the crisis struck, or, if possible, to help him achieve a higher level of ego-functioning. In the case of chronically malfunctioning people and long-term social pathology, like poverty, the last best balance would be hard to find indeed, and in such situations one could not use crisis intervention because the situation would not be a crisis in the first place. Before we leave these attributes of crises that are applicable to the practice of crisis intervention, it is important to comment upon the fact that there are objectively determined crises that do not upset some people, and there are mild occurrences that are perceived by others as crises, although they would not appear to be terribly severe. We all know people who rise to emergencies and cope best in a crisis, and we also know people who fail at the first sign of a strong wind. Thus our diagnostic assessment must be of the person in his situation, not merely of the state of crisis or of the person's coping capacity. Crisis theory is by definition a transactional theory in that the crisis has both its objective determination and its subjective response to the state of emergency or loss.

Crisis intervention theory draws specific implications for social work practice. Among its most important guidelines is the fact that practitioners must be accessible and available, preferably at locations where the crisis might occur, but at the least, ready to spring into action as close in time and place to the occurrence as possible. It means that waiting lists are dysfunctional, that taking life histories before helping is no longer necessary, and that all possible measures must be taken to make rapid diagnostic assessments of ego-functioning in the crisis and of the adaptational balance previously achieved so that the helping goal will be immediately apparent.

STRATEGY AND TASK

In a study of social work practice in a prison, Studt reports in what will probably be known years from now as a "seminal article,"[149] an approach to help of prisoners that cross-cuts all methods in social work. As we have already discussed the question of general vs. specific practice in Chapter 1, we will address here the substance of Studt's article, her use of the concept of task and strategy planning, for it has a strong bearing on the case we are trying to present in this book.

We have set up certain requirements of help that derive from the modern social scene. Among these are that the person to be helped must participate fully in the process, because this is an age where little else is left to individuals except the mastery of their own life goals, and this has to be protected at the very least by social work practitioners. Studt recognizes the problem when she asks whose goal determines how various tasks will be related to each other. Is the agency to assume that its social mandate defines goals of action? Or is the worker to rely on his professional

---

[149] Studt, *Op. cit.*

expertise, his values, and knowledge to take the lead in focusing the goals for the client? Studt suggests that "the worker achieves his professional goals through the client's presentation of his." In other words the social worker and client will have common goals with different tasks allocated for reaching those goals. In Studt's view, the worker must provide the conditions necessary for the client to carry out his tasks; the worker functions through indirect actions, while the client does what he must do as a primary responsibility in direct activities. It is evident that only the individual himself can accomplish the tasks required of his life stage and particular situation. "This distinguishes between imposing professional values as experts, with the client as recipient of services, and real self-determination." As demonstrated by Studt, this conceptualization of practice is professional help in accordance with the client's natural life style and unique commitments, as opposed to the intervention of the professional expert in causal ways to change the client's life.

The practice model that Studt suggests is "making a situational analysis and planning appropriate intervention strategies, establishing and guiding over time in each case a set of working relationships among task-related persons . . . regardless of method." The description of this model takes in many of the characteristics of the model we have been attempting to devise in this book. In Studt's article, to which we have been referring, as in the work of Cumming and Cumming,[150] Schwartz and Schwartz,[151] and William Caudhill,[152] in psychiatric hospitals, she proposes a model of organizational behavior that would give expression to her practice model. She speaks of "people working together instead of employing experts to do something," and she comments upon the need for social workers to have a responsible

[150] Cumming, Elaine and Cumming, John, *Ego and Milieu,* Atherton Press, New York, 1962.

[151] Schwartz and Schwartz, *Op. cit.*

[152] Caudhill, William, *The Psychiatric Hospital as a Small Society,* Harvard University Press, Cambridge, Mass., 1958.

role in the agency which will give them the freedom of movement to create practice situations that will affect the client's conditions. She sees a pooling of functions and their flexible use to support the work of the clients in managing their own tasks. This is surely a difficult model to fit into the typical hierarchical one usually found in bureaucratic structures. Such a model would require a total relaxation of statuses to provide for different kinds of intervention called for by the immediate situation. It would require a downward and outward delegation of authority, so that client need, rather than agency manual and administrative decision, would determine the plan of action. It would require a design for free flow between and among personnel, client and administration, so that participation and feedback would be built into the structure. In other words, a modern view of social work practice would make it necessary to change the traditional view of organizations before it would ever be possible to provide a meaningful social work service.

We have made some comments upon the changing social scene in the urban community, the necessity for participation of clients as citizens in their own self-help. The professional expertise rests in precise diagnostic understanding of the person in situation and in knowing how, where, and under what conditions to allocate personnel and facilitate a plan of action. But none of these can occur while the practitioner and the client are bound by archaic agency structures.

In the first place, Studt does not confine her model to traditional modes, but relaxes it to apply to a transactional, existential situation; she wants to locate the problem, the issue at hand, and to provide all of the exigencies necessary to deal with it. The problem, defined in person-in-situation may be comprised of individual people, dyads, triads, group, or institution in its spatial boundaries, all of which might be potentially obstructive or enabling in an individual case of psycho-social dysfunction. This is an organizational strategy, and as we have tried to show, individuals interact with organizations at all steps in their lives. One can hardly diagnose the person separately from the situation; thus, as the diagnostic process has come to include large parameters to study, these are the components that need to be treated or helped.

In examining the task and situational strategy approach, we must inevitably deal with organizational factors that form the other half of the person-in-situation configuration. For, the social work practitioner as "agency in action" will be carrying out functions that the agency is set up to provide, and both worker and agency, like all aspects of social institutions and city structures, become connected with the individual's behavior.

OTHER MODELS OF SOCIAL WORK PRACTICE

In the search for relevance, mental health and social work literature have described theoretical developments and practice experiments that all seem to be reaching for similar aims. Such interventive modes as group treatment, family treatment, and milieu therapy reflect the movement toward systemic thinking, for the broader the unit of attention the more are systemic variables included in the case boundaries. Furthermore, when the unit of attention includes those people and situations which are in the individual's transactional field, the focus on the here and now and on reinforcing the balance of forces in the case becomes paramount. The greater the number of variables attended to in the case, the greater the chances of effective intervention.

We have said that the chief aim of the social work practitioner is to individualize, to sort out "the case" from the mass. As the parameters of "the case" become enlarged to include variables in the individual's transactional field, proper diagnosis will enable the practitioner to determine where in the total field intervention is needed in order to restore balance or equilibration between the person and his significant social situation. This mode of practice would appear to be well-suited to the urban society, for it is congested and at the same time isolating; people suffer from its restraints even while they seek reinforcement from its institutions.

The social work practitioner, if located at those sites where people go in the normal course of their lives, could fulfill the need of humanizing or individualizing the urban environment. All people need to be touched by another person while they move through the increasingly bureaucratized urban environment. Most people need help in negotiating that environment, in learning about its resources and how to use them. Some people need help in advocating for their rights to services. The urban strain is demanding, and there is no single cure for all of its ills; it is a meaningful aim to contribute as a social work practitioner to the easement of that strain and to the enhanced coping of the individual in his struggle to survive anonymity.

Clearly, if social workers are to move into the life of the community and be available at the potential developmental stress points where people are, there will have to be a major revamping of the use of social work manpower. Mastery of this difficult issue will probably be the key to the continuing usefulness of social work in this country. Everything we have said about coverage, inclusion of large numbers of people as consumers of social work services, and attention to the broad transactions of individuals in their environment suggests that a vast army of individualizing practitioners will be necessary to carry out the mandates of this form of practice. In the next and concluding chapter we will look at the possibilities for differential uses of manpower that would suit the purposes of greater individualization in the urban environment.

7

an approach to the differential use of social work manpower

It is generally agreed that the central problem of modern society is the integration of differentiated activities into some kind of meaningful and coordinated whole. Among these differential activities are occupations, or occupational roles. It is the emergence of occupational roles which more than anything else distinguishes modern society from the folk type.

——Walter I. Wardell[153]

---

[153] Wardell, Walter I., "Social Integration, Bureaucratization, and the Professions," *Social Forces*, May 1955, p. 356.

ANY VIEW OF THE ISSUE of manpower in a field of practice must depend upon one's perception of the aims and practices of that field. Thus, in the area of social work, were one to assess its purpose as being mainly to treat in hopes of curing clinically diagnosed individuals and families within traditionally structured social agencies, then one would need to count the pool of professional social workers and relate this number to the best estimate one could make of potential clients. Where there was a disparity between supply and demand, one would either attempt to expand the numbers of professionals to meet the need or restrict the numbers of clients to places available in each agency. This mode of coping with manpower shortages is a familiar one; it accounts, in part, for waiting lists, for restrictive intake policies, for expedient and unplanned short-term treatment schemes, and sometimes for group treatment. Where these policies and practices are used as accommodations to the shortage of professional staff and not as utilitarian in their own right, then they may reflect the effort in the field of social work to get around the manpower shortage without changing the fundamental structure of services or aims of practice. Another example of the way in which the field has attempted to deal with the "numbers game" related to the professional manpower shortage has been to exert strong efforts to increase the numbers of professional workers through provision of more graduate schools of social work, larger classes, more scholarships, modified programs, and other devices for expanding numbers.

As we have seen in our previous discussion in Chapters 1 and 2, the field of social work is in a critical state, suffering from its own identity crisis and from attacks from the community at large. It has seemed that while psycho-social need, particularly in the cities, has been getting out of hand as far as the quantity of demand is concerned, social workers who are limited in numbers have been increasingly less able to meet that demand. Moreover, we have noted that the nature of the demand for service has changed markedly and that in many instances social work practice has been unable to adapt to new strains in the community. Despite the gradual appearance in the last decade of these fundamental challenges to the practice of social work, nothing has shaken the field as much as its belated recognition that it was running out of professional manpower. Despite very early warnings, it was not until the middle 1960s that the manpower question got into the mainstream of the social work literature, conferences, reports, and research. The dilemmas proposed by the shortage of manpower possibly have been salutary, because they have literally forced the field to re-examine its practices and purposes. It seems to have been a roundabout way to rethinking social work practice, but it served the immediate purpose of coming to terms with reality. Manpower shortages are not what is wrong with social work practice, but if the pressure of staff needs has opened up the field for review, then it has been a valuable problem. In any case, a manpower strategy must be part of the total reconceptualization of social work practice; the lack of such a strategy in the past surely contributed to the practice dilemmas in which the field presently finds itself.

THE EXTENT OF THE PROFESSIONAL SHORTAGE

The gap between supply and demand of professional social workers is distributed unevenly among fields of practice, with public welfare agencies accounting for proportionately fewer professionals than other settings.[154] According to an estimate made by HEW, there were 12,000 professional vacancies in 1965 and a projected 100,000 by 1970.[155] Naturally, increasing demands for social work

[154] National Social Welfare Assembly and U.S. Dept. of Labor, Bureau of Labor Statistics, *Salaries and Working Conditions of Social Welfare Manpower in 1960*, National Social Welfare Assembly, 1961, p. 1: "Caseworkers reporting some study in graduate schools of social work were more prevalent in State or local voluntary agencies (3 out of 5) than in State or local government agencies (1 out of 4)."

[155] *Closing the Gap in Social Work Manpower*, Washington, D.C., Dept. of HEW, 1965.

services will continue to widen the gap, particularly when social work jobs are defined as requiring professional manpower. The deficiency may be even greater than official estimates describe it, for many unfilled staff positions go unreported, either because of a sense of hopelessness about recruiting staff or because administrative actions are taken to reduce services or speed them up as an accommodation to the lack of staff, and thus the unfilled positions become more or less invisible. A major contributing factor of the professional manpower shortage is that about 60 graduate schools of social work produce approximately 3500 professional graduates a year.[156] Clearly, it is presently a statistical impossibility for graduate education to keep up with the ever-increasing gap between the supply and demand for professional social workers. Finally we must keep in mind that these estimates of shortages apply to current conceptions of social work practice; were the field to assume the stance about individualizing practice that we are discussing in this book, and were professionals viewed as the typical practitioner, the gap between supply and demand would be so phenomenal a solution would, indeed, be out of sight.

SOME CAUSES FOR THE GAP BETWEEN SUPPLY AND DEMAND

Apart from the obvious factors that we have noted as causes for the professional manpower shortage, the increasing demand and the proportionately small supply of graduates, there are other reasons that account for the problem. Barker and Briggs[157] and others have made careful, well-documented statements about the *lack of a manpower*

---

[156] National Association of Social Workers and Council on Social Work Education, *Your Stake in the Social Work Manpower Crisis,* 1966.

[157] Barker, Robert L., and Briggs, Thomas L., *Trends in the Utilization of Social Work Personnel: An Evaluative Research of the Literature,* N.A.S.W., New York, 1966.

strategy in social work that finds expression in at least three ways:

1. Professional workers are *unevenly distributed,* so that some fields of practice that may be in the greatest need of them are often the ones that have least of them; some fields of practice actually have too many professionals for the scope of the service they offer, while other fields cannot attract and hold professionals. This competition is too often governed by parochial factors rather than by client need.

2. All kinds of social work manpower, professional and nonprofessional, are *not used differentially,* in accordance with their particular knowledge and skills. Thus professionals may be underutilized and nonprofessionals may be overutilized. This lack of functional clarity makes for waste of available manpower in a tight employment situation that can ill afford it.

3. *Inefficient practices* also waste valuable professional manpower, when tasks are not reviewed or reconstructed in light of manpower realities and newly defined approaches to "the case." Some examples may be seen in cases that remain in treatment for years, without focus and without end; in cases where social workers do tasks that are best performed by the client himself or an organization in his community, in cases where referral and intake procedures require repetition of the exploratory process; in cases where immediate intervention in the environment rather than treatment interviews would not only be more appropriate but more saving of worker effort.

Thus the manpower shortage could be viewed as a symptom of dysfunctional case and staff practices; it is a problem that is larger than the issue of numbers, and it requires solutions that transcend the issues of increased recruitment for professional education and more equitable deployment of staff among fields of practice. The manpower issue itself has become a rather convenient scapegoat within social work, where it is often heard that "if only we had more staff, money, faculty, space, training supervisors, time, etc.," the job could be done. We will attempt to demonstrate here that the manpower issue is systemically related to the traditional social work scheme of services, and the problem is circular. There is a manpower shortage because the field of social work continues to pursue an outworn mode of practice, and because it pursues an outworn mode of practice, there will always be a manpower shortage.

SOME IMPLICATIONS FOR PRACTICE

One of the most serious effects of the manpower shortage upon even the most sophisticated and refined practice is that it may actually distort the accuracy of a diagnosis or the appropriateness of a treatment plan. This is not simply because nonprofessionals might make a mis-diagnosis, or because professional staff is hurried or overworked and therefore might overlook significant factors in the case. The problem is more complicated and has something to do with the residual nature of social work practice. Where a case is defined in clinical terms and there is a severe shortage of treatment resources (due, in large measure, to the manpower shortage), the diagnosis and treatment plan will often reflect this reality. As an example of this negative kind of self-fulfilling prophecy, let us assume we know the all too typical case of a black adolescent boy who has been adjudged delinquent and is in need of a residence of some kind. Although we are not here designating whether the residence ought to be treatment-oriented or health-promoting in its program, the boy in our case example is known to be unable to return to his home and must go somewhere, hopefully where he will be helped to cope better with his life. Further, assuming that the reasonable alternatives indicated for this boy might range from a treatment kind of residence to a carefully selected foster home, a protected boys club, or a state school with limited facilities for delinquent boys, can we imagine where he would finally go? Because of limited facilities, the boy might not fit into the programs of any of the prescribed residence programs, either because he is of a minority group, is too old or too young, is too aggressive or too passive, or is too sick or too well psychologically. It is not uncommon that an accurate diagnosis, which would demand an appropriate resource for him, would sooner or later become masked by the impossibility of getting him to the facility he really needs. So a disturbed boy who needs X treatment center will sooner or later be viewed as perhaps not so disturbed, because the only residence available to him is the state school, or lacking even that resource, review of the case might finally indicate that he is able to go back home after all.

Practitioners all know cases where similar accommodations to shortages have had to be made. There are cases where the prescribed treatment, arising from an accurate diagnosis would be full psychoanalysis, hospitalization, group therapy, or casework treatment, but primarily as a result of manpower shortages, none of these treatment resources are available. Often, in such cases, first-aid measures are used as a compromise or as a holding action. Thus the main purposes of accurate diagnosis and careful treatment planning are bypassed; practitioners become discouraged; agencies become defensive; and the client in question may actually be misled. Unless there is a miraculous narrowing of the gap between supply and demand of professional manpower, reality itself must force the field of social work to reconceptualize its practices, so that clients are more appropriately served.

There is a second deleterious effect upon the nature of practice itself that derives in part from the manpower shortage, and it appears in this instance that the shortage serves some latent function for the field. Obviously, where lack of professional staff is a major administrative problem, therapeutic programs will be devised for increasingly smaller groups of clients. Thus, depending upon the availability of workers skilled enough to do the job, intake policies must accommodate to this reality by becoming increasingly exclusive. The potential client group might become only those who are "treatable" or "workable" or those people who are "able to use the services of the agency." However the lines of eligibility are drawn, whether around treatability or motivation, problem classification, or even ethnic group or class affiliation, the agency's services must be restricted. This will not only mean that increasingly fewer people will be served but also that practice will become increasingly residual. With personnel shortages an agency can ill afford to reach out into the community for more cases or place their intake process much further back on the interventive scheme to reach people earlier in the course of psycho-social breakdown. The shortage of professional manpower might even appear as a justification for restriction of services, and this very restriction itself serves as justification for providing strictly clinically based, therapeutic programs. The ultimate result of this residual direction of social work programs is that practice could literally paint itself into a corner and finally into oblivion. While the urban condition calls out for individualizing services, professional social workers who might be best qualified to provide these services become further and further removed from the scene.

PROPOSED SOLUTIONS

The purpose of this book has been to suggest an approach to social work practice that would be relevant to the modern urban crisis. In the attempt to redefine the boundaries of "the case" and to envision practitioners carrying out early interventive individualizing tasks somewhere in the person's unique transactional field, we have pointed out the changes necessary as to where social workers would need to be located, the aims of help, and how the practice model might be viewed in systemic rather than clinical terms. This effort to reconceptualize the purposes of social work practice comes out of the conviction that the time is overdue and that urban populations are in danger of becoming lost in the bureaucratic maze; our proposal has not been suggested as a solution to the manpower shortage. Yet a strategy for the use of manpower is an essential part of the proposal of a different model of practice. Obviously, if the therapeutic model cannot be sustained with manpower arrangements now existing, it would be ludicrous to imagine that a much broader conception of practice would be effective with the same kind of manpower strategy. The therapeutic model of social casework practice *requires* that a professional worker be the therapeutic agent for every case. We have established that the scope of the case has widened beyond the one-to-one ratio of worker to client, and presently caseworkers in their practice include dyads, triads, families, and groups, where the aim of casework is treatment. It must follow that the best treatment would occur only where the worker was professionally skilled; any use of nonprofessional workers, therefore, would be an *accommodation* to the unfortunate reality that there is a shortage of professionals.

However, were the social work practice model which we have described to be followed, a professional worker would not have to be the primary therapeutic agent mainly because therapy would not necessarily be the primary purpose in the case. Our systemic view of "the case" would make provision for a nonprofessional worker to intervene at various intersections, not as a compromise but as a diagnostically determined first-choice worker who would be used to carry out that task to which he is the best suited.

Given the assumptions about a systemic model of practice, the role of the professional practitioner would be one of accountability for but not necessarily of direct action in every case in his assignment load. If the professional worker were located in an emergency service of a large hospital, he might be allocated the responsibility for the entire population of the clinic, or if it is a very crowded clinic, he might share with any number of other professionals a proportion of the clients for whom each would be responsible. A "caseload" then might number into the hundreds, but there would be unlimited numbers of various kinds of nonprofessional personnel available to carry out the bulk of the case related tasks. Theoretically, at the point where professional social workers assume the multiple roles (which are all part of the practice role) of case consultant, diagnostician, case planner, sometimes a therapist or an advocate, and leader of the social work team, there could be a sufficient supply to actually cover the total "client population" defined by an agency program. We might even see the day when total neighborhoods are thus attended to, when all the residents of a housing project are known, when every person who must go to a hospital is touched in some way by the individualizing social work service. When manpower no longer serves as a restraint upon social work service, it may be possible to move all of practice back into the sphere of early intervention before psycho-social breakdown. But the subject of differential use of manpower is very complicated, and it is important to consider it in detail, so that all of its dimensions are laid bare.

DIFFERENTIAL USE OF MANPOWER

Nonprofessional social work personnel are called by many titles, and there are always implications that are broader than the titles themselves. The main point, however, is to keep in mind that our discussion will relate to *differential* use of professional and nonprofessional manpower, for where nonprofessionals are viewed as substituting for, as less than, or as preparatory to professional status we will have missed the point entirely. It might bear repeating here, that the assignment of tasks to nonprofessional social workers is not to be construed as an accommodating measure because there are not sufficient professionals to go around. Moreover, nonprofessionals cannot be expected to perform the same tasks as professionals, and as we view the use of various kinds of manpower as a permanent condition of social work practice in the urban scene, nonprofessionals will need to have an integral career line that is comparable to that of professionals. This career line should not necessarily lead into the professional line, except through continuing education, but should have its own direction and goals.

As we are using *professional* as the pivotal concept, i.e., professional vs. nonprofessional, we need to affirm that which the professional is characterized by. In light of the fact that graduate education is a requisite for professional knowledge and skills, it is important to understand just what it is that the social work graduate student learns in school that cannot be learned on the job or through life experience. To the degree that there is a component of professional knowledge that is currently only available through formal education, the differentiation among personnel will be easier to assess. The typical curriculum in a graduate school of social work includes study of social and behavioral sciences, social policy, research and theory and practice in one or all of the major social work methods. The scope of these areas of knowledge is broad enough to understand the person-in-situation field, including the range of life styles and problems most commonly met in practice and included in the social welfare structure. The knowledge base of practice, of course, is the major factor that differentiates a professionally educated social worker from an agency-trained worker.

The theory of practice itself provides for a broad repertoire of roles and techniques, making the graduate worker mobile as he selects appropriate measures of help in each case situation. That a graduate social worker is not "trained to tasks" nor oriented to a single setting but rather is educated to generalize his practice through many kinds of functions, across the boundaries of social institutions, with a variety of people, is the chief differentiating factor between that graduate and the nongraduate worker in social work. The professional hallmark is a broad base of knowledge applied with skill within the structure of a theoretical framework of practice. Professional education contributes to the individualizing process, because it provides the practitioner with multiple lenses through which he views cases, thereby increasing the chance that the individual will not be perceived in too narrow a cast. Briefly stated, the current mode and content of professional education for social work actually is suitable to the view of the individual in his transactional field; the professionally educated social worker should have the diagnostic framework and range of interventive techniques necessary for individualization in the modern urban society.

DEFINITIONS OF NONPROFESSIONAL SOCIAL WORKER

All terms assigned to a group of people carry implications about their significance. A common name given to those personnel who work in a field of practice, but are not actually professionals of the field is *paraprofessional.* Meaning "along side of," the concept is clear, that a worker of some nonprofessional status works along side of a professional worker. Although the term is quite dignified and thus has particular usefulness, it may perhaps be too dignified in social work, where the tasks of workers in both statuses have not yet been delineated. In contrast to medicine, where the term paraprofessional actually designates a person who has a specific paramedical function, a paraprofessional in social work seems to lend more social distance to the concept than would be desirable; it is perhaps a bit pretentious for the present status and functions of both the professional and the nonprofessional social worker.

At the other extreme, the title *nonprofessional,* although accurate, says not too much but too little about the worker. Although it is a purely descriptive term, it nevertheless carries a connotation of a nonsomething. It doesn't specify any kind of task, it is too diffuse in its meaning, and, most serious as an objection, it creates a polarity between professional and nonprofessional statuses. It might even seem to place the "nonprofessional" worker out of the social work system altogether.

The term *subprofessional,* of course, has an even more negative connotation and would always signify that such a worker was less than someone else. This designation would not contribute toward the goal of team work and would undoubtedly create more difficulties than a title ought to do.

Another common title that has somewhat demeaning implications is *aide*. This signifies an assistant or a helper, and although a professional worker might, indeed, have several kinds of aides, clerical, administrative, and mechanical aides of one kind or another, the term does not really explain the meaning of the worker who carries out his own integral functions in a case. A term that has served as a compromise in recent years had been *preprofessional*, but like aide, it carries the implication that the professional status is the most valued, and that the preprofessional worker is only waiting until he is able to transfer to the professional status. Whereas in individual instances this may occur, the use of the term preprofessional merely helps to postpone the day of reckoning; the preprofessional may actually remain in that state permanently. In any case the tasks he will expect to perform ought to require an affirmative title that actually denotes a status of its own.

Having thus dispensed with all terms that are para, non, sub, and preprofessional, as well as with the aide that is assistant to the professional, we need to consider the possible, affirmative job titles that come closest to explaining the nature of the person's job and provide for him a career line and a sense of purpose for the job itself, in its own right. Such a term is social work *technician*.

There are several types of nonprofessional social work personnel who have specific functions in the field of social work, but who are not ever perceived as social work technicians; a nonprofessional working in social work might actually be a professional in another field, like a psychiatrist who would have a specific treatment or consultative role in a case, but would not be doing a social work technician's job at all. Another example of a nonprofessional person who often is involved collaboratively in a social work case is a homemaker or a foster parent, each of these adjunctive workers having assigned tasks that are significant to the welfare of the individuals in the case, but none being defined as social work tasks. A further example of nonprofessional and nontechnician personnel may be found in institutional or milieu staff; cottage parents and arts and crafts teachers carry out defined functions that are not construed as social work, although they perform within the boundaries of the social work case. All of these kinds of professional and semiprofessional categories hold in common the fact that they each have their own specialized knowledge and functions, their own career lines, and their own reference groups. Although they are often vital to the conduct of case actions and may work within the aegis of a social work agency, they address the system of the case through other means than social work practice.

On the other hand, the social work technician would be viewed as a member of the team that has as its major function the individualization of people in the urban environment. The technician would not only be integral to the total social work function but also would have his own career line and appropriate tasks assigned to him that could reflect the total social work scheme of intervention. The concept of the team is particularly useful when one views the case in systemic terms for, as we noted in Chapters 5 and 6, the transactional field that radiates from the individual is full of opportunities for intervention on many levels; there are potentially endless numbers and kinds of vital tasks that need to be carried out in all social work cases, and these tasks, defined by professionals, could be allocated to technical workers. Recalling that the systemic view of the case provides for early intervention in accordance with the client's life-style, when we consider the possible tasks, we will be able to account for very wide use indeed of the technical social worker's skills.

Still considering the definitional aspects of the career technician in social work, his educational background theoretically could range from high school dropout to college graduate. If professional competence is seen to derive from knowledge gained in graduate school, then it would be important to relate the technician's level of education to the tasks he is expected to carry out. Thus a social work team might include a professional who would be responsible for the whole course of intervention in a case, a college graduate who might differ in the kind and quality of tasks he carries out from the high school drop-out worker who might also be on the team. As the spread of educational level increases, it will be necessary to assign even more carefully tasks that are relevant to the competencies of the workers.

A word ought to be mentioned about the *indigenous worker*, whose characteristics are often confused with educational characteristics. Indigenous actually means "native to," and thus an indigenous worker might be a college graduate who lives in a certain neighborhood and is selected for the social work team for exactly that reason. An indigenous person might be an ex narcotics addict who serves as a helping person in a group of addicts, or he might be a member of the ethnic group that is the unit of attention for the ubiquitous social work team. An indigenous worker may be of any educational background, and his special skill will be his intimate connection and knowledge of the client group that is being served. He may play a vital part as a member of the social work team, as a bridge between the team and the neighborhood, as interpreter of needs, or as neighborhood entrepreneur. As we shall try to point out later when we discuss the varied tasks of professionals and technicians, the indigenous worker could be a valuable social work technician, and as such he would have to have a career line to pursue.

We have cited the various kinds of personnel potentially available for social work intervention on a massive scale. However, there are many hard questions that will have to be dealt with before technicians can be drawn into the organization of practice in social work. Can career lines be guaranteed? Can technical tasks be sufficiently gratifying to warrant careers? Can meaningful tasks be defined and teased out of traditional professional functions? Can professionals find sufficient rewards in indirect treatment and the assumption of consultative roles? Can the total social work function be defined?

APPROACHES TO DIFFERENTIAL USE
OF STAFF IN SOCIAL WORK

There are some systematic studies of staff utilization in social work[158] but far too few that devise a conceptual scheme and control the input and output so as to assess the relative merits of various kinds of models. Many approaches to the subject describe informal, individual agency experiments that have usually evolved from pressures of the manpower shortage. Although it is understandable that in the frantic race to close the gap between supply and demand of professional manpower, most social agencies work alone at their own expedient accommodations, the fact remains that there can be no accommodating solutions to the problem without fundamental changes in practice itself. Despite the fact that these changes have not been occurring with noticeable rapidity, it might be clarifying to review and evaluate the ways in which the field presently differentiates between professional and technical staff functions in social work.

---

[158] There is increasing literature on the matter of manpower strategies, and the following citations highlight some representative ones:

Barker and Briggs, *Op. cit.*

Brieland, Donald, *Differential Use of Manpower for Foster Care in a Public Child Welfare Program,* Dept. of Child and Family Services, Springfield, Ill., 1964.

Epstein, Laura, "Differential Use of Staff: A Method to Expand Social Services," *Social Work,* Oct. 1962, pp. 66–72.

Heyman, Margaret, "Criteria for the Allocation of Cases According to the Level of Staff Skill," *Social Casework,* July 1961, pp. 325–331.

Richan, Willard C., "A Theoretical Scheme for Determining Roles of Professional and Non-Professional Personnel," *Social Work,* Oct. 1961, pp. 22–28.

Schwartz, Edward E. and Sample, William C., "First Findings from Midway," *Social Service Review,* June 1967, pp. 113–151.

1. THE CASE AS THE UNIT OF DIFFERENTIATION

This may be the most common factor of differentiation, but it has severe drawbacks as a classificatory scheme mainly having to do with the underutilization of professional knowledge and skills, and a corollary overutilization or inappropriate use of technical knowledge and skills. To assign cases to one or another level of staff, it would be necessary to define the cases as simple or complex, healthy or sick. This would be almost impossible to assess without adequate diagnostic knowledge. Thus the professional practitioner would need to be drawn in some fashion anyway in every case, in order to make that assessment. Where cases are differentiated according to the degree to which they reflect inner and outer problems, or emotional vs. concrete need, this approach tends to dichotomize the case in ways that are antithetical to the conceptualization of social work cases as psycho-social, and of individuals as pivotal in their fields of transaction. In a word, it is not possible in a systemic approach to the case to divide the case up into inner and outer need, for there is an intrinsic relationship between both aspects of the person-in-situation configuration.

2. THE TASK AS THE UNIT OF DIFFERENTIATION

The idea of a fixed, specific unit of work to be exacted from a practitioner has certain attractive possibilities, because if it were possible to predefine such tasks it would be relatively easy to allocate them appropriately and to train technicians in their use. The difficulty with this approach is that tasks in social work generally go in clusters, and they are not without implications for more complicated work. For example, making a school visit is hardly a defined task, when there are unaccounted variables that are involved in the process. Another problem with the assignment of tasks to technical workers is that they often are the menial or residual tasks that professionals do not want to do in cases, and thus they may be unrewarding for the technician as well. Finally, when some tasks are too preciscly predefined, they tend to be rather concrete and their value, as well as their drawback, is that they tend to require repetition. This will make for a certain kind of rigidity in the work and ultimately in the process of carrying it out, so that it soon becomes a meaningless and routine gesture in the total conduct of the case. The client would then be ill-served, and the technician would soon be bored and disinterested.

3. WORKERS' QUALITIES AS THE UNIT OF DIFFERENTIATION

This is a common approach to the problem of allocating the case assignments in social work, but it does not relieve the burden of the necessity to close the manpower gap. The differentiation is actually made at the time of recruitment and selection of staff, when an assessment is made as to the particular expertise of the professional and the non-professional worker. Professionals are assumed to have special qualities in knowledge and skill arrived at through education, and nonprofessionals are selected for their personal qualities and experiences. Then, depending upon the needs of the case, that staff member who is "best suited" to carrying out the treatment tasks is assigned to the case. Clearly, this is an approach that requires the least effort in clarifying the job to be done and in rearranging the patterning and functioning of staff.

4. ORGANIZATIONAL FACTORS OR THE UNIT OF SERVICE AS
    THE DIFFERENTIATING UNIT

In this approach, professional and technical staff are assigned differentially to the *location* in the agency where certain types of problems are expected to appear, and it is assumed *a priori* that those problems will require one or the other level of skill in practice. Thus in public welfare agencies it has been common to assign nonprofessionals to the places where public assistance checks are to be allocated and professionals to the locations where "personal problems" are to be handled. This approach is similar to the case, task, and worker differentiating schemes, and carries the same disadvantages. There is always a great deal of functional overlapping when cases or problems of individual clients are divided up for administrative reasons, and more importantly, as the core practice component in social work is the diagnostic, individualizing assessment of "the case," the *a priori* assumption of level of skill needed tends to sidestep the real issues in the manpower dilemma.

5. CLIENT VULNERABILITY, WORKER AUTONOMY SYSTEM OF DIFFERENTIATION[159]

This is a more sophisticated approach to the differential use of staff, because it comprises more than one variable and accounts in some measure for the multi-dimensional client-worker interaction. The approach is interesting, but it has some of the same drawbacks that we have noted in the other schemes, particularly in regard to the initial assessment of client vulnerability. In order to determine the degree of client vulnerability, a professional worker would need to be involved directly in every case, in order to make a proper assignment to the right staff person. Another concern that this approach raises is that the assessment of vulnerability and complexity, by whatever standard, might tend to once again as in the days of clinical preoccupation lead toward a hierarchy of client troubles which would inevitably impinge upon worker status and ultimately create a new form of residual service. As far as the notion of worker autonomy is concerned, this would be a more fruitful direction to pursue, were there not such a wide range of worker competencies in both the professional and the technical sphere. The field of social work is presently hard put to assess the relative skills of a recent professional graduate who is up-to-date in knowledge and a graduate who has been practicing for many years without educational refreshment. As far as technical staff is concerned, as they will not have been "pre-tested," as it were, in graduate school, and as by their nature, they would represent

---

[159] Richan, *Op. cit.*

the universe of possibilities as far as personality characteristics and knowledge and skills are concerned, the degree of worker autonomy would be difficult indeed to assess.

6. EPISODE OF SERVICE APPROACH TO DIFFERENTIAL USE OF STAFF[160]

This approach is the latest, most highly refined, and sophisticated scheme yet devised for differential use of social work personnel. It provides for flexible boundaries in regard to the kinds of service given, groups of cases, and teams of professional and technical workers. In other words, the approach is not tied to narrow considerations that would relate only one worker to one case, or to a definition of a single task. The maneuverability of the *episode of service* approach is its great asset. It is intricately related to the *goals* of the service, and the means used by the social work team to arrive at the goal would derive from the requirements of reaching that goal and the available skills of the team members. It is "any cluster of activities which must go together in order to achieve a given goal . . . it includes . . . all the alternative means by which to achieve it."[161] According to Barker and Briggs, "The means chosen are those which the workers are competent to perform," and there are vast arrangements possible to provide for an array of competencies, so that infinite kinds of skills could be made available to the client. The differentiating scheme lends itself very well to a reconceptualization of practice and an imaginative use of combinations of professional and technical social work manpower. We are almost ready to discuss a model for an appropriate utilization of manpower in a developmental approach to social work practice in the urban community. First, it is necessary to deal with the special case of the indigenous worker and the associated issue of careers in social work for nonprofessional personnel.

---

[160] Barker and Briggs, *Op. cit.*
[161] *Ibid.*, Table III.

THE INDIGENOUS WORKER IN SOCIAL WORK

There is a fast-growing body of literature citing studies and experiences about the increasing use of community people in social work and mental health services.[162] Understandably, there is a tendency to overdraw the values of wide use of indigenous people for one or two reasons. In the first place, as we have noted in our earlier discussion about the practice of social work, it is a field that often appears to the public to be based upon the neighborly application of common sense. Naturally, if sensible friendly visiting were all there was to it, and if citizens are becoming fearful of the increasing institutionalization of their personal lives, then there would be a sense of relief in knowing that neighbors or at least people in the same situations as they could be as helpful, if not more so, than an organizational representative like a social worker. This tendency to seek the most informal and parsimonious solution to a problem is as natural as wanting an aspirin to do the work of more complicated medical procedures. As a matter of fact, in accordance with our interest in patterning practice in light of the natural life style of clients, the aim of informality and parsimony or economy of treatment procedures is a very respectable practice goal.

The assumption that indigenous personnel can better perceive the needs and required services of people in the

---

[162] The following materials are illustrative of the work being done in the area of indigenous workers:

Barr, Sherman, "Some Observations on the Practice of Indigenous Non-Professional Workers," *Personnel in Anti-Poverty Programs,* Council on Social Work Education, 1967, pp. 51–61.

Birnbaum, Martin L. and Jones, Chester H., "Activities of the Social Work Aides," *Social Casework* (Special Issue on Project Enable), Dec. 1967.

Pearl, Arthur and Reissman, Frank, *New Careers for the Poor,* Free Press, New York, 1965.

Specht, Harry, *et al.,* "The Neighborhood Sub-professional Worker," *Children,* Jan.–Feb. 1968.

community has been thoroughly explored in at least one examination of the subject.[163] As Barr evaluated the popular notions of the special advantages in using indigenous personnel, he dealt with several common dictates that were found wanting. For example, in response to the idea that indigenous people are more like other members of the community, Barr pointed out that this is not necessarily so, because in the case of Mobilization for Youth (MFY) it was noted that the people who served as workers were actually more successful and upwardly mobile than their neighbors and that in their aspirations toward middle-class values they tended to be better educated and managed their lives better. One could cite similar possibilities in an indigenous group of alcoholics, where the very success of the man who would have controlled his addiction and attained a helping role would set him apart from the others in the group. Barr concludes that it is not possible to generalize about the indigenous person's special knowledge and skill in conceptualizing community needs, but rather that it is important to select community helpers in accordance with their individual personal qualities. Thus a potentially helpful indigenous person would be one who was warm and friendly or especially knowledgeable about the subculture of his neighborhood and not a person who qualified merely by happening to be indigenous to the neighborhood.

Barr cites another common overgeneralization about the indigenous person being a more acceptable model to the client group than the professional social worker. He challenges this idea in light of the fact that the indigenous worker often tends to be harder on his neighbors than a professional person, in his effort to prove that he is not naive or able to be manipulated. The assumption that the poor worker is perceived as more helpful to the poor client than is the middle-class worker not only is not always true, but, in fact, if the perception does exist, neither is it accurate. The middle-class or professional worker ought to be

[163] Barr, *Op. cit.*

more knowledgeable about community resources and how to bring them to the client's need, and his middle-classness need not necessarily be an obstacle, *as long as need is met.* Barr points out that the one time in which the indigenous person is probably more useful as a role model is prior to the client's engagement in the social work service, or at the time of intake, when he does not trust the social worker because he does not trust the system from which he comes. This issue is an important one today, in light of the increasing division of races in the urban scene. Are we prepared to affirm that only a black person can be perceived by other black people as helpful? In the beginning, perhaps so, but help is not necessarily defined according to racial lines; the level and content of the help ultimately will determine its value.

A third assumption about the special value of indigenous worker is challenged by Barr when he questions the idea that they have special competency because they "have been there" and know best how to negotiate the system. Barr points out that, in the case of MFY, this knowledge was actually quite specialized and limited in scope. It is one thing to know how to reach a public assistance worker on the telephone and quite another to know how to cope with the intricacies of a large welfare bureaucracy and confront it on the correct level of abstraction, using the most meaningful language.

Barr affirms the existence of certain qualities of style that are less formal, less distant, and more "directive, partisan and active," which were characteristic of their indigenous workers. This matter of style is something that professional social workers might try to emulate in light of their interest in working with groups of clients who are of different class or ethnic affiliations than they. Yet there is more to practice than style and partisanship, for without knowledge of the facts and meanings of a case, no amount of passion and activism can assure the client the kind and quality of service he requires. Barr further agrees with other experts on the subject in his view of the bridging function of indigenous personnel, where they serve as connections between the social organization and the community. The indigenous bridge may connect class with class, race with race, professional with client, and ultimately service with need. The caution presented by Barr is against romanticizing the effectiveness of the indigenous worker. Professionals can learn a lot from working with them and they have unique tasks to perform, but to overstate their qualities and affirm their use as substitutes for the professionals is to beg the question of how to narrow the manpower gap and provide more relevant services to people in the cities.

The *second* major reason that seems to underlie the current pressure to expand the use of indigenous workers is because it is seen as an employment opportunity for unskilled people, and therefore a way out of poverty. We have discussed the transition from an industrial to a service employment market, where trade skills have had to give way to managerial and personal qualities. This change in the employment market has contributed to the very serious technical unemployment of people who are already socially and educationally disadvantaged. The fields of social work and mental health services have been the logical sources to which society has looked for mass employment of technically unemployed people. As long as one keeps in mind the fact that employment of the poor through social work services is not identical with the giving of services, one can explore the possibilities without being tyrannized by a fallacious outcome. We are not saying here that full employment is not one of the most important ways out of poverty, for it most certainly is just that. Rather we are saying that even if there were infinite jobs to be filled by poor people in social work, the filling of these jobs could not be equated with service of quality. We have just cited some of the reasons for this, in that we assume that there are more requisite knowledge and skills in the practice of social work than can be taught to or applied by indigenous workers who have not been through the educational experience that provides those requirements. To the extent that we keep separate the two goals of excellent social service and full employment, we can explore the potential market in social work services for the employment of poor people.

The employment market for indigenous workers in social work is probably unlimited; as unlimited as is the potential sphere for social work services at large. When we discuss the realignment of staffing patterns and the differential allocation of tasks in our conceptualization of social work practice, we will see that the indigenous worker might necessarily become a significant member of all practice teams. When staff positions are apportioned carefully, when there is a manpower strategy, there will be an important place for indigenous workers. It is impossible to know at this time if the places potentially available for some poor people will make even a dent on the rate of unemployed people in the cities of this era, but the view of developmental social work services that addresses the client's transactional field will certainly provide for enhanced use of personnel of various kinds more than the clinical model of practice could ever entertain. However, it is not sufficient to open up job possibilities for whatever purpose, unless there is a clear vision of the career line a person might follow. People need to be promoted, not only in terms of job titles, salary levels, and other signs of real or imagined status, but also in terms of the variety and complexity of their jobs. The matter of "New Careers" is a crucial issue that has to be confronted before wild employment takes place; the next steps need be foreseen before the first ones are taken.

ISSUES IN CAREERS FOR TECHNICIANS: GUIDELINES FOR THE DESIGN OF NEW CAREERS

In an excellent monograph,[164] Sidney Fine has differentiated between the worker who holds a job and the

---

[164] Fine, Sidney, *Guidelines for the Design of New Careers,* The W. E. Upjohn Institute for Employment Research, Kalamazoo, Mich., Sept. 1967.

trainee who is on a step in a career ladder. The special qualities of a career job rest in the educational atmosphere in which the worker is trained, where mistakes are treated as learning opportunities, where he is given some degree of freedom in carrying out his tasks, and where the tasks are used as the basis of increasing knowledge. Fine also contributes a distinction between the *prescribed* and the *discretionary* content of a job. The former type of content is defined by the supervisor, sets limits on the means by which the work is to be done, and holds out certain expectations for results. The latter content is decided by the person doing the job, and there is the expectation of use of judgment, where the trainee chooses his own alternatives at each stage. The proper combination of both of the kinds of job content undoubtedly would clarify the specific work expectations for technical social workers. The most important point made by Fine is that tasks themselves do not have prescribed or discretionary content. For example, making a school visit or referring a person to a clinic are tasks, but different aspects of the how, why, when, and what way of carrying out those tasks are both discretionary and prescribed. The ideal aim in developing career lines for any type of personnel is to increase as far as possible the discretionary possibilities in all job functions. The hallmark of professionalism is exactly that of wide discretionary powers; whereas the limits of discretion may be narrower for the technician, some discretion must be possible or the growth of a career will not be realistic. In other words, the career technician must be able to look forward to increasing responsibility both in the scope of his job and in the opportunities to make judgments and select alternative means of carrying out his job.

In order to achieve the goals of closing the manpower gap, of providing a vast array of individualizing services, and utilizing professional and technical social work personnel, it is evident that the first decisions that need to be made will have to do with the definition of practice, and *the delineation of tasks and functions.* The second set of decisions will have to be about how to *increase worker autonomy* through relating worker skills, knowledge, and experience to the job to be done. Related to this is the necessity to formulate a model of staff patterns that would accommodate the professional and technical social work team concept. Each set of tasks that are allocated to the technical person will, of course, modify the functioning of the professional person. Needless to say, promotional opportunities, personnel practices, salary levels, and provision of in-service training still will be essential components of any plan to revise the social work system to include responsible use of career technicians with professional social workers.

In determining the kind and content of career lines in social work, we come back to the same need to re-examine the purposes of social work practice. Changes in manpower arrangements, as adaptations in knowledge of human behavior and social science and modifications of practice models, all require revision of the aims of social work. Changes cannot be pasted on to old conceptualizations, for all changes, when viewed systemically, affect and are affected by the content and the purposes of the job to be done. When "the case" is viewed in its transactional field, the work to be done is addressed to that field, and the essential tasks are then allocated across the varied manpower dimensions. Conversely, if we were to make such a statement from a manpower point of view, we could say that the manpower shortage is such that the field of social work must devise formal arrangements for technical staff to divide the work with professional staff. This will inevitably modify the clinical model of practice, for psychotherapy cannot be carried out by nonprofessionals and the job must somehow be redefined to make use of different job skills. Again, we might arrive at a similar conclusion through the route we have taken in this book.

Beginning with the assumption of the need for individualization in the urban scene, we must confront the issue of spreading the services of organized social work manpower. In order to achieve this aim, it is necessary to reconceptualize "the case" and to find imaginative ways of using differential manpower so as to be effective in intervention in the individual's transactional field. Wherever one starts, the conclusion is the same, because all of social work knowledge, techniques, values, objectives, manpower uses, and practices themselves are components that are systematically related to each other.

SOME APPROACHES TO DIFFERENTIAL USE OF MANPOWER IN TEAMS

In assuming that the professional-technical social work team is the most flexible model for the differential use of manpower, there are within that model, several ways of allocating the tasks to be done.

I. THE PROFESSIONAL AS SUPERVISOR OF TECHNICIANS

This is a common approach, used quite often in social agencies like public welfare departments where there is a preponderance of nonprofessionals who carry the major direct practice function in the agency. "Saving the professional" for supervision does not necessarily contribute to raising the level of direct practice, because the technician must carry the whole case and thus has an almost unlimited range of discretionary control over his actions and the direction of the case. The responsibility for the diagnostic assessment is his, as well as for the range of interventive techniques. Lack of educational qualification in this instance would tend to make the case ill-served, for the technician could not, without a framework of knowledge, correctly assess the individual's total psycho-social situation and his need. Administrative arrangements, manuals, written policies, staff training courses or supervisory conferences can only define the boundaries of the technician's practice; they cannot substitute for formal professional education. Where the professional is used in this way as supervisor, he tends to oversee staff and not cases. Thus the quality of practice must rely upon the accident of the quality of staff available, and the client can have no assurance of direct expert attention.

2. THE PROFESSIONAL AS CONSULTANT ON CASES

This approach copes better with the issue of providing direct expert attention to the individual client. When the supervisory function is carried out by a senior staff person, it might tend to be more administrative, and thus more capable of being filled by an experienced technical worker who has *come up the career line.* The professional would be "saved" for the tasks he is most qualified to carry out, the *thinking tasks* for which he has been educated. We have said that the diagnostic assessment of a case is a high-level task that requires specific knowledge of the psychosocial configuration. The decision about what is out of balance in the case is the pivotal determinant that finally calls all interventive tasks into action. If there were only one senior brain surgeon in the only hospital in a city, difficult dilemma though it is, it might be a more judicious use of his time and his skill to "stand behind" the resident surgeons, making the diagnostic assessments of the brain damage, and directing the hands of the resident surgeons who would wield the surgical tools, than to operate himself on only a tiny proportion of the patients in need of surgery. The social worker as consultant would be directly involved in the vital diagnostic and treatment decisions in all cases, and the technician would carry out the direct interventive or treatment tasks.

3. THE PROFESSIONAL AS TEAM LEADER

Here the professional would enter into direct practice, carrying out difficult functions in cases and utilizing technicians either as specialists in particular tasks, or as the "arms and legs" of the professional in every case. The matter of the *technician as specialist* can be illustrated by imagining a pool of workers, each of them having an area of expertise achieved through life experience or staff training. For example, one worker who might be a college graduate could become expert in making referrals to homes for the aged; he would need to know a great deal about the referral process, but perhaps even more about the resources for the care of the aged in his community. As he built his knowledge of the subject, became acquainted with the staffs and programs of the various homes, etc., he soon could enjoy a rather large measure of autonomy or discretionary control over his work. The important point is that while the technician gains expertise in home finding, the professional retains control of the treatment planning in the case. Depending upon the setting or field in which the team is located, technical specializations can be defined in any area of life that is relevant to the clients' potential needs. Thus, one might assign an indigenous member of the team to case and problem finding in the neighborhood, another technician team member to supervision of children in foster homes, or to aged persons who are housebound. The task assignments could be as varied as the kinds of cases there are; the two principles to be observed in this form of staff utilization are that the professional is responsible for every case, and the technical worker achieves expertise in carrying out one or more tasks that are repetitive in many cases. Thus the professional can carry many more cases, because he has access to the unlimited pool of expert technicians who can be drawn in to carry out defined tasks. The opportunities for staff advancement should be apparent, because the technician would be able to achieve increasing levels of expertise in his field of competence, ultimately arriving at the top of the career ladder where he might supervise other technicians who are working in his area of competence.

The other kind of team arrangement to which we have referred is the kind where the technician serves as the "arms and legs" of the professional, not as an expert in a pool of experts, but almost as an aide to the professional. In this arrangement, the professional might have one or more technicians assigned to him who would carry out a variety of tasks as called for in each case. Although this approach has the advantage of variety and less chance of routinization of work, it does not offer quite the same opportunity for the technician to rise on a career ladder parallel to the professional. This is because the professional would retain supervisory responsibility for all of the tasks on the case, and the technician would not necessarily achieve competence in a particular pursuit.

Whichever of these approaches are utilized, the professional as team member would be able to increase his span of work, serving more people and reaching out into the client's entire field of transaction.

It is too early in the development of manpower models to assert which kind ought to be utilized in a particular field of practice, but there are unlimited possible arrangements that can be imagined. The following is an example of a plan for the use of professional and technical manpower that reflects all that we have been discussing in this book. Let us imagine a large city hospital located in a ghetto area, where people use the emergency clinic much as middle-class people might use a private doctor's office. Actually, due to the fact that mechanical aids are becoming essential in medical care, because there is a shortage of doctors, and because medical specialization requires group medical practice, the use of general clinic resources is increasing in all communities, no matter the level of income. Although middle-class people might still have private doctors, it happens increasingly that doctors ask their patients to go to the nearest clinic, so that they can have access to the whole range of medical resources. Assuming then that the local general or emergency clinic will serve as a typical resource for the catchment area peopled with the entire range of medical problems, such a location would be a perfect place to test out the social work practice model which we have been addressing. Where the hospital becomes an institutionalized part of the life of the community, like the local community center or the social security office, we are no longer dealing with a residual conception of service. Social work services would have the opportunity to be located where people are and where they are pursuing their natural life styles and encountering the crises of life with differing degrees of coping capacity.

While the accompanying chart is addressed to the scene of a hospital in the ghetto, it might also be addressed to a variety of like communities such as neighborhoods, tenant's groups, schools, and the host of social utilities and other social institutions that we discussed in Chapter 4. There are several principles to be drawn from this design, among which are two that are particularly significant. In the first place, the entire "population" (in the instance of our illustration, every person who attends the clinic) would be accounted for, or touched in some way by a social work technician who would be the individualizing arm of the institution in question. This screening action connotes *opportunity* for advocacy, information, and a broad range of help. The choice as to the use of the help would be the person's, for the primary service (in this case, medicine) would be available for him whether or not he needed or wanted social work intervention. Second, the primary case decision functions would rest with the professional social worker, related to the technician more or less as head of the team, or at least as consultant on case actions.

As the threads of our proposal have become woven together, the whole cloth of social work intervention in the modern urban scene is before us. The "case" will be an individual in his field of transaction. Social work practice intervention is conceived as sufficiently broad-ranging, flexible, and relevant to the needs of people that it can be called into play wherever in the client's field there is imbalance. A variety of social work personnel who would carry out a yet-to-be-defined host of tasks would be available as integral and necessary within the social work interventive scheme. The professional social worker then would apply his knowledge and skills appropriately in both diagnostic and treatment areas, and the client-citizen would be met in his own unique milieu. Were such a preventive design

A. *Case Finding*

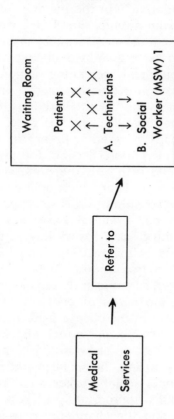

Technicians meet everyone in the waiting room and bring Patient Data to MSW*, who makes a diagnostic assessment of need.

There are several *dispositional options* available to the professional social worker at the Clinic:

1. Mark NO CASE MADE.

2. Assign case to Social Worker (MSW) 2, for interview to clarify situation.

3. Assign case to supervisor of pool of social work technicians for direct action on services requested.

Diagrammatically, this process would look this way:

B. *Initial Disposition*

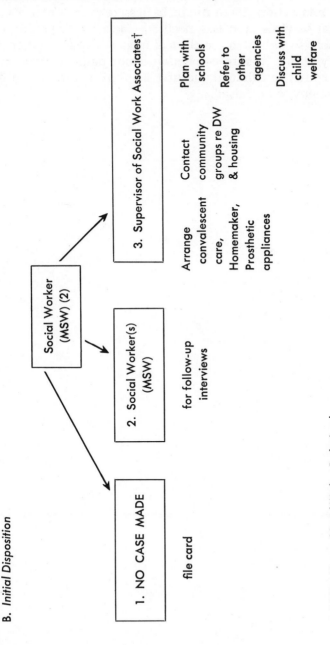

Social Worker (MSW) (2)

1. NO CASE MADE

file card

2. Social Worker(s) (MSW)

for follow-up interviews

3. Supervisor of Social Work Associates†

Arrange convalescent care, Homemaker, Prosthetic appliances

Contact community groups re DW & housing

Plan with schools

Refer to other agencies

Discuss with child welfare

* MSW = Master of Social Work or Professional
† Social Work Associates = Technicians, indigenous workers, aides, etc.

put into action, there might be less reliance upon residual social services, and less need for social work practitioners to hold so tightly to the clinical model of practice that must carry with it a sure conviction about pathology and cure: the conviction that in the first instance caused the critical questions to be raised.

epilogue

WE HAVE TRIED to connect social work practice with our view of the way the world is turning. F. S. C. Northrop observed that "at the initiation of inquiry one must question every traditional belief"[165] simply because there is a problem. He suggests that there are only normative social theories, that one asks "what might be the case, not what is the case," as in descriptive scientific theory. So, as anticipated by Northrop, we have confronted a problem of values.

To the degree that there is validity to our observations, there will be some who will join in our views. Others will feel we have not seen far enough into the future, and still others will want to turn away from the imminent reality and perhaps turn back.

The changes that seem inevitable in the practice of social work will undoubtedly be gradual, despite the clamor and demand for immediate change. It will be necessary to find ways to relate to the present world within the present framework, because changes in organizational structures and in practice modes ordinarily do not occur simultaneously. Despite the inevitable lags in one or another area, we do not have to await the millennium, for practice can loosen up even while it is housed in rigid structures. It is unlikely that organizations will change by themselves without the conviction of the professionals within them. Social workers

---

[165] Northrop, F. S. C., *The Logic of the Sciences and the Humanities*, Meridian Books, The World Publishing Co., New York, 1967, p. 16.

will need to experiment, to demonstrate new approaches to practice, and to evaluate what happens. The choice of path to be followed, of course, will be governed by so many value considerations that the future direction of social work practice cannot be assured. We can but hope that whatever path is taken, people will be served expertly and exactly as they need to be.

index